T0306015

Building a
Responsive and
Flexible Supply Chain

Building a Responsive and Flexible Supply Chain

Yoshiteru Minagawa

Nagoya Gakuin University, Japan

 **World Scientific**

NEW JERSEY · LONDON · SINGAPORE · BEIJING · SHANGHAI · HONG KONG · TAIPEI · CHENNAI · TOKYO

Published by

World Scientific Publishing Co. Pte. Ltd.
5 Toh Tuck Link, Singapore 596224
USA office: 27 Warren Street, Suite 401-402, Hackensack, NJ 07601
UK office: 57 Shelton Street, Covent Garden, London WC2H 9HE

Library of Congress Cataloging-in-Publication Data
Names: Minagawa, Yoshiteru, 1952–   author.
Title: Building a responsive and flexible supply chain / by Yoshiteru Minagawa
    (Nagoya Gakuin University, Japan).
Description: New Jersey : World Scientific, [2018] | Includes bibliographical references and index.
Identifiers: LCCN 2018008588 | ISBN 9789813222090 (hc : alk. paper)
Subjects: LCSH: Business logistics.
Classification: LCC HD38.5 .M563 2018 | DDC 658.7--dc23
LC record available at https://lccn.loc.gov/2018008588

British Library Cataloguing-in-Publication Data
A catalogue record for this book is available from the British Library.

For any available supplementary material, please visit
http://www.worldscientific.com/worldscibooks/10.1142/10493#t=suppl

Desk Editors: Anthony Alexander/Lixi Dong

Typeset by Stallion Press
Email: enquiries@stallionpress.com

Printed in Singapore

Preface

All firms are socially responsible to ensure that their customers are satisfied with firms' products or services. Meeting the challenge of customer satisfaction requires building an integrated and collaborative supply chain that can respond flexibly and quickly to changes in the market demand. Enhancing cooperation along the entire supply chain requires aligning partners' behavior with the optimal behavior of the supply chain.

Firms' sustainable competitive advantages that can distinguish them from their competitors include highly differentiated functions and benefits that customers can obtain through products or services, products or services at affordable prices, conformity to specifications, shorter time for delivery of products or services desired by consumers, excellent after-sales service, and easily accessible distribution channel, and entrenched brand loyalty. To obtain competitive advantages, supply chains must absorb, adapt, and transform flexibly to changes in the market demand. Furthermore, building a flexible supply chain requires a close relationship among partners.

The study reveals accounting-based management control system practices that are conducive to managing integrated and flexible supply chains toward increasing customer satisfaction. Moreover, it explores how supply chain integration can be increased. This study also examines the relevant managerial methods to build the most effective supply chains in each stage of the product or service life cycle. Furthermore, this study explores the appropriate managerial methods of various types of supply chains, including a nonprofit network (disaster relief supply chain).

This book is organized into 10 chapters. The first chapter considers the issues that supply chains should overcome and the managerial theories they can use in achieving customer satisfaction. The second, third, and fourth chapters consider how a flexible supply chain can be built and how it can increase customer-perceived value. The second chapter explores how a significant improvement in break-even time of products or services contributes to customer satisfaction and the accounting-based management control systems that can facilitate shortening the break-even time. The third chapter considers the impacts of mitigating supply chain risk on cooperation among partners and a switching cost-based analytical model for managing flexible supply chain. Moreover, this chapter examines a real options-driven management control system that can alleviate business risks inherent in relationship-specific investments in supply chains. The fourth chapter examines how customer satisfaction can be quantified — in other words, the performance indicators for customer satisfaction — and further creates a balanced scorecard for enhancing customer value in supply chains.

The fifth, sixth, and seventh chapters consider management control systems for the most prominent types of industrial supply chains. The fifth chapter clarifies that the key to winning a competition among fabless supply chains is research and development, and considers how the joint profits of a supply chain should be allocated among fabless firms and electronics manufacturing service providers to strengthen their competitive advantage. The sixth chapter focuses on a relationship among finished products' assemblers and parts suppliers, and examines an appropriate management approach for such inter-firm networks. The seventh chapter explores how a supply chain serving goods at the maturity stage of a product life cycle can outperform competitors and considers throughput accounting-based management control systems.

The eighth and ninth chapters examine cost management and quality control in supply chains. The eighth chapter sheds light on cost management methods in supply chain serving products at each stage in the product life cycle. The ninth chapter discusses quality management along the supply chain. It considers the importance of preventing quality errors, the effects of product design for quality and traceability systems as effective prevention practices, and how quality control practices in a supply chain can be effectively adopted. The tenth chapter discusses a method of self-funding for rapid response operations, where respective participants in humanitarian supply chains determine the contribution they can make according to their own means. Moreover, it addresses the advantages of online fundraising for humanitarian supply chains.

I am very grateful to Ms. Dong Lixi, Ms. Chandrima Maitra, and Mr. Anthony Alexander, in-house editors, World Scientific Company, for their invaluable efforts in making this book a reality. I would like to thank Editage for English language edits.

About the Author

 **Yoshiteru Minagawa** is a Professor in the Faculty of Commerce at Nagoya Gakuin University in Japan. He received his PhD from Nagoya University and is a major in management accounting. He was a Visiting Scholar at the Berkeley Roundtable on the International Economy at the University of California, Berkeley in 1999–2000, and at the College of Business at San José State University in 2012–2013. His current research interests focus on the role of management accounting in supply chains, and customer value-based pricing strategies. His main publications include "Profit Allocation Rules to Motivate Inter-Firm Network Partners to Reduce Overall Costs", in Monden, Y. (ed.), *Management of An Inter-Firm Network*, Singapore: World Scientific, pp. 61–76 (2011); "Management of Humanitarian Supply Chains in Times of Disaster", in Monden, Y. (ed.), *Management of Enterprises Crises in Japan*, Singapore: World Scientific, pp. 149–164 (2014); "How to Facilitate Inter-Firm Cooperation in a Fabless Global Supply Chain", in Monden, Y. and Minagawa, Y. (eds.), *Lean Management of Global Supply Chain*, Singapore: World Scientific, pp. 47–64 (2015).

Contents

Preface   v

About the Author   ix

Chapter 1   Research Framework   1

Chapter 2   New-Product Launch Strategy in Supply Chains   11

Chapter 3   Flexible Supply Chain Management   31

Chapter 4   Supply Chain Balanced Scorecard for Customer
              Satisfaction   47

Chapter 5   Fabless Supply Chains Management   63

Chapter 6   Profit Allocation between Assemblers and Parts
              Suppliers: A Normative Perspective   79

Chapter 7   Management of Supply Chains Fulfilling the
              Demand of Mature Goods   97

Chapter 8   Cost Management in Supply Chains from
              a Life Cycle Perspective   111

Chapter 9   Supply Chain Quality Management   129

Chapter 10   Management of Humanitarian and Disaster Relief
              Supply Chains: Addressing Ways to Raise Funds   145

Index   161

Chapter 1

Research Framework

This chapter will show the primary perspectives on supply chain management.

1. Supply Chain Versus Supply Chain Competition

According to Fisher (1997, p. 107) and Ross (1998, p. 12), supply chains perform two different functions. First, a supply chain has access to customer demand, a piece of information that is shared across all supply chain participants. Second, supply chains enable timely and cost-effective movement of products or services.

In studying supply chain management, it is important to distinguish between internal and external networks. Internal supply networks execute all functional operations in-house. In contrast, an external supply network comprises various separate companies with different strategies and/or agenda. This study examines the management of external supply chains. Although member organizations of an external supply chain establish inter-firm linkages, they simultaneously seek their own specific interests while doing so. It is therefore most likely that some partners will behave in a self-benefiting fashion. In other words, partners will not be enthusiastic about taking unjustified economic risks only for the interest of others (Das and Teng, 1998, p. 504). Therefore, essential supply chain management issues are how to achieve (1) incentive alignment (i.e., aligning the interests of supply chain partners) and (2) goal congruence (i.e., integrating partners' goals into the goal of the entire supply chain).

From planning/development to creation/provision of products or services, it is practically and economically difficult for a firm to perform all business processes independently. Therefore, the enhanced profitability of firms that are responsible for different business operations largely depends on whether their finished product or services can capture high customer value in the market. The more the firms increase customer value for their finished product or service, the more they can increase their share of profits.

In recent years, many industries have witnessed rapid changes in market demand, such as the shortening of product, service, and technology life cycles, and an increased diversification of consumer needs. Thus, the biggest challenge faced by many firms, regardless of the supply chain stages they manage, is to satisfy end-consumers through their finished products or rendered services. Survival in the market environment requires getting all firms engaged in creating, distributing, and selling the finished product or service to operate in a flexible and cooperative manner. One competitive advantage in changing markets is the synchronization of activities along the supply chain to satisfy finished products' customers. This requires information sharing among the channel members.

Thus, the growth of firms depends largely on whether the firms can be part of a well-integrated supply chain. Hence, supply chain versus supply chain competition is getting fierce in many markets.

2. Competitive Cooperation in Supply Chains

Porter (1985) presented the determinants of competitive advantage. In it, the focus is on the tendency of companies belonging to more profitable industries earning bigger profits than those doing business in less profitable markets. In other words, a determinant of a company's profitability is its industry's overall profitability. This argument paves the way for competitive cooperation: the ability of supply-chain-wide collaboration to increase its partners' respective competitive advantages. Thus, promoting cooperation among partners toward increasing the supply chain's overall profit has become a critical issue in supply chain management. There are two approaches in inducing the partners of a supply chain to collectively behave toward increasing the whole supply chain's profit. One is power-centric coercion and another is the linking of the supply chain participants' goals (Maloni and Benton, 2000). This study considers the latter.

An example of a business model that fosters competitive collaboration is revenue sharing among teams in professional sports leagues. For example, Atkinson *et al.* (1988) examined the effects of revenue sharing in the National Football League. The revenue-sharing business model provides a percentage of the teams' revenues, composed of ticket selling and broadcasting revenue, to a shared pool. The pooling is followed by redistributing a percentage of the revenue pool equally among individual teams. An instrument for achieving competitive balance throughout the league is revenue sharing.

However, equitable revenue-sharing schemes embrace a disincentive effect-driven issue (referred to as free-riders). Small-market teams can, relative to their contributing money to the funding pool, get a bigger piece of the overall pie. On the contrary, there is a tendency that bigger-market teams can get a relatively smaller share of the pooled money. Leagues' sustainable growth requires discouraging small-market teams to spare investing money in their own competitiveness. A solution for low-revenue teams' free-rider problems is to set prerequisites to receive the benefit of revenue sharing (Rathbun, 2014, pp. 33–34). According to Rathbun (2014, pp. 33–34), there is a rule setting the minimum before-redistribution revenue required for the individual teams to get a share of pooled money. Another way to cope with the free-rider problem related to the cross-subsidy is to allocate a group's entire revenue or profit among its members per their actual investment or contribution.

3. How to Achieve Goal Congruence among Partners

The key for a supply chain to outperform competitors is to motivate all partners to make fruitful investments that can contribute toward effective and timely realization of potential opportunities for growth (Baiman and Rajan, 2002, p. 213). Che and Hausch (1999) show the following three types of organizational investments. An investment is "selfish" when it benefits the investor. An investment is "cooperative" when it generates direct benefits for the trading partners. An investment is "hybrid" when it has both cooperative and selfish elements (Che and Hausch, 1999, p. 126). Based on Che and Hausch (1999), the study addresses the following two types of supply chain investments. First, every partner must invest to reduce the cost burden on other partners. Second, individual partners should invest capital to satisfy the end-consumers served by the supply chain. These capital investments commonly lead to the expansion of profit or the size of the "pie" of the entire supply chain, thereby increasing each partner's share of the entire "pie".

The potential benefits from capital investments of all partners dedicated to increasing the value of the supply chain's output are reaped when the firm becomes part of the supply chain. However, successful realization of the potential benefit requires encouraging all participants in the supply chain to execute capital investments specifically devoted toward supply chain differentiation. To facilitate such relationship-specific investments across the supply chain, it is essential that supply chains establish incentive alignment schemes aimed at fully motivating all partners to cooperate toward increasing the competitiveness of the whole supply chain and realizing goal congruence. Bouillon *et al.* (2006, p. 265) show two aspects of goal congruence: a manager's voluntary acceptances of an organization's strategy and a manager's consensus regarding the organization's strategy.

According to de Waal (2006), members of a group actively pursue common goals, whose benefits can be attained only through collaboration (de Waal, 2006, p. 349). Furthermore, participants of collaborative projects are also concerned with the division of rewards. Thus, throughout the engagement, participants eagerly compare their efforts and expected rewards to those of the other members of their group. Negative reactions ensue in cases of unfair rewards (de Waal, 2006, p. 357).

The distribution of a supply chain's joint profit among partners is considered a supply chain management practice that aims to strengthen cooperation among all the partners and foster competitive advantages over rival supply chains. A fair rule for distributing supply chain profit among partners is to use the contribution of each partner toward the attainment of the goals of the entire supply chain. Specifically, there are two approaches for quantifying effort levels as the basis for profit allocation. The first approach is referred to as input-oriented measures that involve how much capital each partner has invested to achieve the supply chains' predetermined objectives. The second approach is referred to as output-oriented measures that evaluate the amount of customer value generated by each partner in the markets.

4. Allocation of a Supply Chain's Joint Profit

A method for building sustainable supply chains and facilitating cooperation among their partners is the distribution of the supply chains' joint financial performance to their partners (Monden, 2009). The specific approaches involve profit sharing, revenue sharing, and transfer pricing. The following presents the traits of these approaches.

There are different types of profit-sharing schemes based on the differences in the coverage of expenditures that are subtracted from sales revenues to reach profits in income statements (Chwolka and Simons, 2003). The application of profit sharing in a supply chain requires securing of the transparency of actual costs incurred by partners. Revenue sharing does not face any issues related to cost transparency in terms of calculating revenue.

Under the allocation of a supply chain's joint profit among its partners, a direct proportional relationship can be built between the supply chain's consolidated-profit and its partner's degree of improvement in cost-and-effect. Therefore, the profit-sharing approach in a supply chain is more useful in motivating partners toward increasing the supply chain's overall financial bottom line.

A managerial practice that uses transfer pricing, which refers to pricing for transactions between a supply chain's partners, is a method used to allocate the supply chain's joint financial performance among its partner (Monden, 2009). For instance, it is a method that sets transfer prices in accordance with the market prices of goods being transacted between the supply chain's partners. The transfer pricing method allows a supply chain's partners to decide upon issues concerning intra-network transactions in the supply chain by using competitive arm's length rules that is reflected in the market price (Minagawa, 2016). Moreover, the market price based transfer pricing method can control the supply chains' performance by comparing it with that of their competitors.

5. Supply Chain Management from a Life Cycle Perspective

Strategic thinking from the perspective of life cycle allows managers to identify correctly and systematically the managerial issues that firms face during the individual stages of the product life cycle. Therefore, analysis from a life cycle perspective can give managers an excellent strategy management lens throughout which they can identify what problems must be tackled in each stage of the product life cycle. Focusing on the current life cycle stage of the firms' products, managers can heavily invest managerial resources to resolve the problems and successfully move to the next stage of the product life cycle (Greiner, 1972). Moreover, Monden (2015) pointed out the importance of Product Life-Cycle Management (PLM) in formulating supply chain strategies.

Using a questionnaire survey, Miyajima (2017) studied Japanese small- and medium-sized enterprises' business policy planning from a life cycle perspective. He examined how often variance levels between actual versus planned performance are calculated: monthly, quarterly, biannually, or annually. According to his questionnaire results segmented by life cycle stage (i.e., growth, maturity, and decline), the highest percentage of firms selecting "monthly" was the "growth stage" group. Contrarily, the highest percentage of firms selecting "annually" was the "maturity stage" group (pp. 69–70). The result is most likely attributed to the fact that firms in the growth stage of product or service life cycle need to pay relentless attention to the influence of rapid changes in market demand on firms' business management performance. This leads the growth stage group to perform variance analysis more frequently than those in the maturity stage. Besides, it is theoretically perceived that firms in mature markets do not require frequent warnings to monitor external competition and competitors continually because mature markets witness less change in each company's market share. Instead, firms facing saturated demand for their products or services need to develop their next star products or services.

6. Customer Satisfaction

Kaplan and Norton's concept of the balanced scorecard shows that a key driver of high profitability in organizations is greater customer satisfaction (Kaplan and Norton, 1992). The achievement of high customer value requires organization-wide, effective, and timely responses to changes in customer needs; and this can be achieved through a focus on intangible assets (Kaplan and Norton, 1992).

Essentially, a strategy formulation process involves making decisions as to what kinds of customer satisfaction to target, and then how to achieve them. To do this successfully, it is essential to determine how to measure customer satisfaction, which will be examined in the study.

Importantly, organizations need to deal effectively with how to gain greater returns from capital investments through in customer satisfaction. Pricing based on customer value is set not on the costs incurred, but on customers' willingness to pay for products' functions. This leads to avoidance of overpricing and underpricing. Overpricing or underpricing occurs when a firm sets the prices of its products or services too high or too low relative to the prices that customers are willing to pay. By assuming that the customer has a good understanding of the value of the products or services, pricing according to customers' willingness to pay greatly reduces losses due to underpricing and overpricing (Hinterhuber, 2004, p. 776).

7. Supply Chain Flexibility

Lee (2004) identified three key factors that can enable supply chains to attain sustainable competitive advantages. The first is the ability to adjust the supply chain's design to meet the structural shifts in markets (Lee, 2004). Next is agility, or the ability to react promptly to sudden changes in demand or supply (Lee, 2004). Finally, the third factor is concerned with the alignment of supply chain partners' interests (Lee, 2004). Introduced by Lee (2004), adaptability, agility, and alignment are the core components of supply chain flexibility (Tang and Tomlin, 2008).

It is important for supply chains to gather and share information on changing markets and customer demands to succeed in changing and adapting their strategies. It is thus imperative for supply chain partners to align incentives and goals. The study sheds light on how to reduce break-even time on new product launches in supply chains. To attain the research objectives, the study explores how robust cooperation among supply chain partners contributes to profitable product introductions. Furthermore, the study examines how the distribution of the supply chain's joint profit among partners can contribute toward the alignment of incentives among partners.

8. Switching Supply Chain Partners

As mentioned above, the application of life cycle analysis to supply chain management helps in the identification of issues that must be addressed to achieve sustainable growth. Managerial issues include strategies that must be formulated and implemented to survive the new products' or services' launch competition during the growth stage of the product or service life cycle, and how to explore new business opportunities during the postmaturity phase of the product or service. Supply chain managers facing these decisions need to consider whether to change or keep members. Based on previous research, a long-term relationship with members contributes toward fostering cooperation (Ganesan, 1994; Vanneste *et al.*, 2014). Therefore, the study will show managerial practices that enable making good decisions concerning switching partners.

References

Atkinson, S. E., Stanley, L. R., and Tschirhart, J. (1998). Revenue Sharing as an Incentive in an Agency Problem: An Example from the National Football League, *The RAND Journal of Economics*, Vol. 19, No. 1, pp. 27–43.

Baiman, S. and Rajan, M. V. (2002). Incentive Issues in Inter-Firm Relationships, *Accounting, Organizations and Society*, Vol. 27, No. 3, pp. 213–238.

Bouillon, M. L., Ferrier, G. D., Stuebs Jr. M. T., and West, T. D. (2006). The Economic Benefit of Goal Congruence and Implications of Management Control Systems, *Journal of Accounting and Public Policy*, Vol. 25, No. 3, pp. 265–298.

Che, Y.-K. and Hausch, D. B. (1999). Cooperative Investments and the Value of Contracting, *The American Economic Review*, Vol. 89, No. 1, pp. 125–147.

Chwolka, A. and Simons, D. (2003). Impacts of Revenue Sharing, Profit Sharing and Transfer Pricing on Quality-Improving Investments, *European Accounting Review*, Vol. 12, No. 1, pp. 47–76.

Das, T. K. and Teng, B. S. (1998). Between Trust and Control: Developing Confidence in Partner Cooperation in Alliances, *Academy of Management Review*, Vol. 23, No. 3, pp. 491–512.

de Waal, F. B. M. (2006). Joint Ventures Require Joint Payoffs: Fairness Among Primates, *Social Research*, Vol. 73, No. 2, pp. 349–364.

Fisher, M. L. (1997). What is the Right Supply Chain for Your Product? *Harvard Business Review*, March–April, pp. 105–116.

Ganesan, S. (1994). Determinants of Long-Term Orientation in Buyer-Seller Relationships, *Journal of Marketing*, Vol. 58, No. 2, pp. 1–19.

Greiner, L. E. (1972). Evolution and Revolution as Organizations Grow, *Harvard Business Review*, Vol. 50, No. 4, pp. 37–46.

Hinterhuber, A. (2004). Towards Value-Based Pricing — An Integrative Framework for Decision Making, *Industrial Marketing Management*, Vol. 33, No. 8, pp. 765–778.

Kaplan, R. S. and Norton, D. P. (1992). The Balanced Scorecard: Measures That Drive Performance, *Harvard Business Review*, January–February, pp. 71–79.

Lee, H. L. (2004). The Triple-A Supply Chain, *Harvard Business Review*, October, pp. 102–112.

Maloni, M. and Benton, W. C. (2000). Power Influences in the Supply Chain, *Journal of Business Logistics*, Vol. 21, No. 11, pp. 49–73.

Minagawa, Y. (2016). How to Facilitate Inter-Firm Cooperation in a Fabless Global Supply Chain, in *Lean Management of Global Supply Chain*, edited by Monden, Y. and Minagawa, Y., Singapore: World Scientific, pp. 47–65.

Miyajima, Y. (2017). *Core Value Driven Management Control System in Japanese Small and Medium-Sized Enterprises*, Doctoral Dissertation, Nagoya Gakuin University, Nagoya, Japan.

Monden, Y. (2009). *Inter-Firm Management Control Based on "Incentive Price": A "Profit-Allocation Scheme" for Inter-Firm Cooperation*, Tokyo: Zeimu Keiri Kyokai.

Monden, Y. (2015). Lean Management of Global Supply Chain: Dynamic Combination Model of Market, Product Life-Cycle, Product Design, and Supply Chain, in *Lean Management of Global Supply Chain*, edited by Monden, Y. and Minagawa, Y., Singapore: World Scientific, pp. 3–46.

Porter, M. E. (1985). *Competitive Advantage: Creating and Sustaining Superior Performance*, New York: Free Press.

Rathbun, S. M. (2014). *An Investigation into the Accounting Practices of Owners in the Professional Sport Industry with Specific Consideration of Implications to Players, Taxpayers, and Local Governments*, Syracuse University Honors Program Capstone Projects, Paper 776.

Ross, D. F. (1998). *Competing Through Supply Chain Management: Creating Market-Winning Strategies Through Supply Chain Partnerships*, New York: Chapman & Hall.

Tang, C. and Tomlin, B. (2008). The Power of Flexibility for Mitigating Supply Chain Risks, *International Journal of Production Economics*, Vol. 116, No. 1, pp. 12–27.

Vanneste, B. S., Puranam, P., and Kretscmer, T. (2014). Trust over Time in Exchange Relationships: Meta-Analysis Theory, *Strategic Management Journal*, Vol. 35, No. 12, pp. 1891–1902.

Chapter 2

New-Product Launch Strategy in Supply Chains

1. Introduction

How do building and participating in supply chains enable firms to boost their profits? Highly integrated supply chains can help firms respond to market changes at optimum speed so that participants can meet end-consumers' requirements cost-effectively. Most industrial sectors must cope with frequent, drastic changes in end-consumers' preferences and requests. Therefore, how to satisfy consumer needs for finished products or services swiftly and at low costs is the most challenging issue for firms throughout the supply chain. Parts suppliers must effectively and efficiently meet consumer needs for finished goods produced by an assembler using their parts. This strategic scenario also applies to retailers seeking to improve their performance by supplying goods in the right quantities and at the right time to the consumers. Retailers who fail to provide consumer satisfaction will not achieve sustainable growth.

Firms are facing a challenging business environment marked by a shrinking product life cycle and thus need to become more flexible and agile in responding to changes in the demand for finished goods. To meet this business agenda, firms must build or participate in supply chain networks to achieve higher levels of customer satisfaction. The strategic values of supply chains lie in the effective fulfillment of functions that foster customer satisfaction (Ross, 1998, p. 12).

Highly integrated supply chains can enable the sharing of detailed information about end-consumer needs among partners, enabling them to cope with market changes quickly and effectively. Moreover, focal firms in well-coordinated supply chains can reassign functions or roles to those partners who are best positioned to perform them quickest and at the lowest cost (Ross, 1998, p. 12). Furthermore, participants in competitive supply chains can easily exploit others' expertise and knowledge. These capabilities allow supply chain partners to compress the time-to-market (TTM) for a new product or service that customers want and reduce the time lag between the placing and delivery or satisfaction of an order.

Shorter break-even time (BET) for new products is currently the most significant success factor in a firm's growth. Supply chain functions namely, the effective sharing of information and knowledge among participants and the transmission of information and products or services enable the effective and efficient satisfaction of consumer needs. Thus, firms participate in a supply chain to achieve their own growth by creating higher levels of customer satisfaction.

Competition is clearly no longer a company-versus-company matter but is increasingly a supply chain versus supply chain one. Such supply chain-based competition is becoming fiercer. One of the ways to create a highly integrated collaborative partnership across the supply chain is to motivate partners to act in the best interests of the overall supply chain through inter-firm, network-wide information transparency on how many of the competitive performance goals have been achieved at any point. Information sharing in supply chains also allows partners to ascertain the extent to which the objective of establishing or entering supply chains has been achieved. This study addresses BET as a supply chain competitive performance measurement.

Hewlett-Packard employs BET to manage new product development (NPD) projects (House and Price, 1991), and represents the elapsed time from the initial spending on product development to the point when net operating profit (sales less cost of sales) equals the total cost of design and development.

The rest of this chapter is organized as follows. The next section carries a literature-based explanation of the underlying theoretical concepts of this study. Section 3 examines how BET can be improved by applying value-based management practices.

2. Literature Review

2.1. Supply chain collaboration

Simatupang and Sridharan (2005) present a framework for analyzing the interaction among supply chain collaboration features. The framework consists of five features of collaboration: a collaboration performance system (CPS); information sharing; decision synchronization; incentive alignment; and integrated supply chain processes. They define collaboration as the close cooperation among autonomous business partners engaged in joint efforts to effectively meet end-customer needs at lower costs (Simatupang and Sridharan, 2005, p. 258). Simatupang and Sridharan (2005) describe the five features as follows.

A CPS is the process by which performance metrics are devised and implemented to induce improvement in overall performance by supply chain members. Mutual performance objectives reflect the competitive factors that can be attained if the supply chain members build cooperation. These factors increase each chain member's profitability (Simatupang and Sridharan, 2005, p. 262).

CPS obtains data about the progress of collaboration and performance status through information sharing and uses them to create new targets and performance metrics relevant to new situations (Simatupang and Sridharan, 2005, p. 263). Decision synchronization includes reallocating decision rights to synchronize supply chain planning and execution to match demand with supply (Simatupang and Sridharan, 2005, p. 264).

Incentive alignment in a supply chain refers to the sharing of costs, risks, and profits among participants, so they are motivated to act consistent with their mutual business performance objectives. It helps motivate members to align their actions to the mutually beneficial purpose of collaboration, which enhances their individual profits (Simatupang and Sridharan, 2005, p. 265). Integrated supply chain processes refer to the extent to which the members design efficient supply chain processes that can deliver goods to end-customers in a timely manner at a low cost (Simatupang and Sridharan, 2005, p. 265).

2.2. Customer value

For all firms and supply chains, one of the most serious challenges is offering the best response to market changes by listening to the voice of the market (Johne, 1994). A sound understanding of customer value allows the formulation and implementation of business strategies aimed at satisfying customer demands.

According to Woodside *et al.* (2008, p. 9) and Best (2009, pp. 95–108), the customer's perceived benefits of goods include benefits from the functionality; service benefits, such as ease of use, repair, and ease of installation; company or brand benefits (e.g., the feeling of satisfaction arising from the goods of competent companies); and emotional benefits (e.g., the ability of goods to make the buyer or user feel good by buying and using them).

Macdivitt and Wilkinson (2012, pp. 13–15) propose three elements of customer value. The first is increase in revenues accruing to the customer from the purchase and use of the products or services. The second is cost reduction by using the products or services. The third is emotional contribution via the "feel good factor," such as stress reduction, peace of mind, increased confidence, and greater safety.

According to Woodside *et al.* (2008) and Macdivitt and Wilkinson (2012), the consumer's perceived value of goods involves several benefits and gains. The first is the benefits arising from the functionality and effects of the products and services purchased by customers. The second relates to benefits arising from services other than the functionality and effects of the products and services. The third is making customers feel good.

Based on the studies discussed above, the detailed descriptions and value drivers of these three consumer-perceived benefits are as follows:

(1) Customer benefits arising from the functionality and effects of the product or service
These include four specific customer benefits and their value drivers. The first is the product's functionality per se and the service effect itself (Woodside *et al.*, 2008, p. 9; Macdivitt and Wilkinson, 2012, p. 14).

This benefit is perceived by customers when the products or services offer emergent functionality and innovative effects the customer has never experienced before. The second specific customer benefit arises from the quality of the products or services (Woodside *et al.*, 2008, p. 9; Macdivitt and Wilkinson, 2012, p. 14). This benefit is recognized by customers when the quality level is higher than expected. The third specific customer benefit results from the economic efficiency of the products or services (Woodside *et al.*, 2008, p. 9; Macdivitt and Wilkinson, 2012, p. 14). The customer benefit's drivers include reducing usage cost, decreasing repair costs, and minimizing loss due to discontinuation. The fourth specific customer benefit is ease of use, which reduces the cost and time required to learn how to use a product or service (Woodside *et al.*, 2008, p. 9; Macdivitt and Wilkinson, 2012, p. 14).

(2) Customer benefits other than the functionality and effects of the goods

These include four specific customer benefits and their value drivers. The first one is easy access to information about the goods (Woodside *et al.*, 2008, p. 9); customers can obtain information and become knowledgeable about the goods through close relationships with the suppliers. The second specific customer benefit is the availability of excellent after-sales services, which is achieved by establishing customer service networks (Woodside *et al.*, 2008, p. 9; Macdivitt and Wilkinson, 2012, p. 14). The third specific customer benefit is ease of order, purchase, and installation (Woodside *et al.*, 2008, p. 9; Macdivitt and Wilkinson, 2012, p. 14). The fourth specific customers' benefit is just-in-time delivery from which customers can deduct forgotten profit caused by slow response to their needs.

(3) Making customers feel good

Comfort can be created when supply chains improve customer satisfaction with services throughout the whole life cycle of products and services (Woodside *et al.*, 2008, p. 9; Macdivitt and Wilkinson, 2012, p. 154).

2.3. Target costing

Life-cycle cost is the total cost of ownership over the whole life of an asset and includes the costs to develop, produce, acquire, use, support, and dispose. A product's life-cycle cost depends largely on the producer, including the facility and technology used (Makido, 1985, p. 128). Almost all production conditions are determined at the design stage of the product life cycle. Consequently, a large part of the costs to be incurred throughout the product life cycle is confirmed at the design stage. Therefore, applying target costing in the development and design stage generates the greatest benefit. Monden (1995) stressed that target costing is a company-wide profit management practice conducted during NPD. Target costing activities include the following: (1) planning products that have customer-pleasing qualities, (2) determining target costs (including target investment costs) for the new product to generate the target profit required over the medium to long terms given the current market conditions, and (3) establishing a product design that can achieve target costs while also satisfying customer needs for quality and prompt delivery (Monden, 1995, p. 11).

In target costing, a new product's cost objective is established from the targeted profit margin determined during corporate profit planning as target cost begins at the product planning and design stage in NPD.

Monden (1995, p. 19) showed that target cost can be determined using either of the following two equations:

$$\text{Target cost} = \text{target sales price} - \text{target sales profit}$$
$$\text{Target cost} = \text{target sales price} \times (1 - \text{target sales profit ratio})$$

According to Makido (1985, p. 130), each new product's target profit margin is derived from the following indicators: (1) its targeted profit margin on sales; (2) competing products' sales prices; (3) the company's past performance; (4) the technological complexity of the new products; (5) a high probability of the commercialization of the new idea embedded in the new product; and (6) a comprehensive technological and commercial evaluation of the new product. Makido's study on target costing practices showed that a targeted profit margin on sales is commonly applied as a criterion for deriving the target cost (Makido, 1985, p. 130).

2.4. Typology of NPD

Booz *et al.* (1982) suggested six main types of NPD: (1) those that provide improved performance over existing products and replace them; (2) those that allow a company to enter an established product market for the first time; (3) those that enable a company to expand its product variety by adding them to its existing product mix; (4) those that create an entirely new market; (5) those that offer performance comparable to that of competing products at lower costs; and (6) those that permit a company to enter new markets (Johne, 1994).

Irrespective of the strategic agenda for the NPD, it needs close cooperation among business partners in the supply chain: these include material manufacturers, components suppliers, assemblers, and marketers with NPD experience who can build new sales channels. It is vital to integrate the expertise of business partners to successfully create new products or services that yield greater or emerging customer values.

3. How to Minimize BET

3.1. Improve performance through supply chains

Upstream and downstream firms in highly integrated supply chains can share information regarding changes in the demand for finished goods (Ross, 1998). As a result, agile supply chain partners can establish an effective value chain for a full range of activities, including research and development (R&D), production, and delivery, which are required to supply goods end-customers want. The chance to acquire this strategic value of supply chains motivates firms to join them and improve their performance.

Thus, supply chains enable quick response to the changing demand for finished goods. How can the competitive advantages of supply chains be quantified? This study clarifies how BET can help motivate supply chain partners to help achieve the chain's competitive advantage.

One of the most significant NPD problems is how to minimize the TTM while avoiding NPD budget overruns. BET is one of the measures that captures the degree of improvement in on-time and on-cost performance for NPD. This information is useful to managers in their decision-making, namely, how to reduce TTM and what is the optimal level of R&D costs, and expected profit from the new products. The following sections present useful management tools for problem-solving using BET.

3.2. Improvement of on-time and on-cost performance in NPD

According to Clark and Fujimoto (1991), the best practices for reducing TTM include overlapped product development and joint R&D between upstream and downstream firms. One of the models for NPD activity is a sequential process in which the downstream activity does not begin until the upstream activity is completed (Krishnan *et al.*, 1997, p. 438). An alternative approach to reducing product development lead time is an overlapped process in which the downstream activity begins before the completion of the upstream activity by using upstream information exchanged in a preliminary form (Krishnan *et al.*, 1997, p. 438). Overlapping product development processes involve the concurrent execution of upstream and downstream activities based on an exchange of preliminary information. The presence of overlapping activities in NPD is conducive to faster product development lead time than in a sequential process (Krishnan *et al.*, 1997, p. 438).

However, the overlapping product development users must cope with an inter-firm relational challenge created due to the use of preliminary information that can cause errors (Krishnan *et al.*, 1997, p. 438). Reducing costs associated with errors requires minimization of fixation time per error, which, in turn, requires early detection and response to problems. Therefore, among the most important success factors in overlapping product development is effective communication and information sharing throughout the networks. How can close cooperation among supply chain participants be established? One of the practical techniques is the allocation of joint supply chain profits among participants, which will be explained later.

Minimizing excess R&D costs yielding no return as well as avoiding costly delays to new product introduction help boost the profitability of products after their release. Constantly executing actual versus planned variance is an effective management approach for motivating new product team members to reduce the time and cost of NPD. The NPD variance analysis process includes setting up an NPD schedule, determining cost targets for the whole life cycle of the project, and monitoring whether the project is proceeding on schedule and whether the actual costs match the planned costs. NPD-variance analysis allows all members of the project to share the goals of NPD time and costs improvement and determine the extent to which the goals have been achieved.

The optimization of trade-offs between time and cost in the supply chain's NPD project is the driver of an increase in the overall supply chain's joint profits (Cohen *et al.*, 1996). Inter-partner collaboration results in trade-off resolution in supply chains. Accordingly, an effective strategy for ensuring that NPD projects are completed on time within the budget, at the optimal trade-off between project time and cost, is the sharing of joint profits among the partners realized through the optimization and driven by supply chain-wide collaboration.

3.3. Value-based pricing

Pricing affects consumers' purchase decision-making, thereby influencing profit margins. Consequently, pricing impacts BET performance. This section explores the effects of value-based pricing approach on BET.

Value-based pricing sets prices based on customers' perception of the value of the products or services rather than on their costs. Therefore, value-based pricing strategies consider how to realize the maximum prices that customers are willing to pay in exchange for receiving benefits from the products or services they have purchased (Liozu *et al.*, 2012, p. 15).

What strategic impact does value-based pricing have on supply chains? First, customer value-driven pricing sends managers the strategic message that customers pay higher prices for products or services as their perception of the value of such products or services increases. Thus, value-based pricing requires managers to create substantially differentiated higher-value products or services. This can result in enhanced customer willingness to pay, thereby boosting net profit margins on sales. Second, value-based pricing considers how to give customers a better understanding of how the companies' products or services are differentiated from those of the competitors. Value-based pricing sets prices principally based on the customers' perceived value. Thus, the more value customers place on the product or service, the higher the price. Value-based pricing therefore results in higher prices. However, the successful implementation of value-based pricing strategies largely depends on effective communication of value to customers (Hinterhuber, 2008).

Thus, value-based pricing, which seeks to create highly differentiated customer value and effective communication of value to the customer, can improve BET in the following ways. Charging prices exceeding customers' willingness to pay adversely affects customers' desire to purchase products or services. High prices inconsistent with customers' perception of value hinder increases in sales, thereby worsening BET. On the other hand, prices lower than what consumers are willing to pay may lead to a low-margin business and reduced profits, which lower BET. To solve these over- and underpricing issues, prices should be set according to customers' perceptions of value. Value-based pricing can increase net cash flows immediately after the release of new products. Value-based pricing, which focuses on customers' perceived values and willingness to pay, reduces lost sales and generates more new cash flow after product or service release (see Figure 2.1).

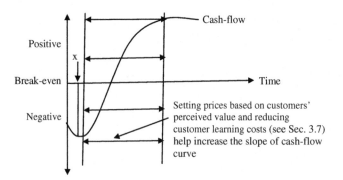

Figure 2.1.   Schematic representation the effects of value-based pricing on revenue
Note: *x* = New product launch point in time.

3.4. Target pricing

Effects of value-based pricing in business are realized through target-pricing and design to price.

According to Makido (2000, p. 169), target pricing involves the estimation of a target price by adding target profits and target costs and then designing a product to realize value that is worth the target price. By analyzing product portfolios composed of both new products to be developed and planned product improvements in the medium- to long-term, corporate managers can determine how much profit they should earn from selling new products. Moreover, corporations can determine target profits for new products and then decide what new products they must design and develop to realize their target profit in the market.

Target pricing research indicates that a strategic question in target pricing for new products is about creating goods that can generate the maximum willingness-to-pay among customers. Managers concurrently adopt value-based pricing too. The target pricing process commences with the development of product concepts that yield customer value worthy of a specified dollar amount. One of the engineering tools used to frame target pricing is design to price (DTP), which seeks to design goods that attract customer value for the target price. Collaborative NPD among supply chain partners, including parts suppliers, assembling makers, and marketers, is a critical success factor in providing more innovative product and service solutions to consumers, thereby enhancing customer value. This means that close cooperation among partners engaged in business operations at each stage in the value chains is indispensable for effective performance of target pricing.

Thus, a core element in target pricing is the integration of market-led knowledge involving customer demand research, product concept planning, utilization, product design, new parts development, parts fabrication engineering, finished product manufacturing, and product marketing. Successful target pricing thus requires effective information sharing among supply chain partners. This means that target pricing practices in higher integrated supply chains yield excellent performance in the development and supply of new products with enhanced customer value.

3.5. Target pricing-driven NPD

This section presents a theoretical description of how to implement target pricing-driven NPD.

(1) Target profits for new products
Business planning involves setting target profits for new products. Target profit setting occurs as follows. First, the overall corporate profit plan for the medium- to long-term is developed. Next, corporate managers analyze their product portfolio comprised of both competitive new product introductions and existing product improvements within the plan timeline, thereby determining projected profits from the sales of new products to be developed.

(2) Identify target product lines and segmentations
Assuming that a firm calculates profit margins on sales for new products to establish the overall profit plans. Meyer and Lehnerd (1977, p. 55) present a high-end versus low-end market segmentation. These two types of products differ in the degree of customer willingness-to-pay. Consumers pay more for high-end products and vice versa. Sales of high-end goods have a significant potential to increase their prices much over their costs, thereby boosting the profit margins. This proves that high-end goods are the best target segmentation for developing goods with high-profit margins on sales. As mentioned, the greater the degree of product differentiation, the greater the customers' perceived value. Consumers are usually willing to pay a higher price for more highly differentiated products. When product purchase prices are at a premium, the company typically earns a higher-profit margin. Hence, it is theoretically possible for targeted profit margin through sales of new products to increase according to the degree of product differentiation.

After determining the amount of target profits that a supply chain must earn through new product launches, it plans and designs new products that yield the planned target profit. Target pricing is the best NPD approach for planning and designing new products with customers' perceived value and thus a potential price premium sufficient to realize the planned target profit goal in the market.

(3) Setting target cost

As mentioned before, target costing establishes the cost objective for new products based on the targeted profit margin on sales determined during corporate profit planning. Medium- and long-term profit plans determine the target ratio of sales cost to sales for each new product. Specifically, the ratio of sales cost to sales is calculated based on the profit margin on sales: target ratio of sales cost to sales = 1 − target profit margin on sales.

Two methods can be used to set the target ratio of sales cost to sales. The first is using a predetermined company-wide target ratio of sales cost to sales as a hurdle-rate applied to individual new products. The second is setting the target ratio of sales cost to sales for each new product according to its level of technological complexity and the degree of product differentiation.

The above calculations result in a target price that equals the sum of the target cost and target profit.

(4) Product design for customer value that worth target prices

Next in the target pricing process, new products that consumers perceive to be worth the target prices are developed. The target typology of the new products using the classification proposed by Booz *et al.* (1982) is determined. Then the new products are segmented. Thereafter, concepts for new products that consumers are willing to buy at the target prices are generated.

After new product concepts are developed, the design stage for the new product begins. At this stage, the concept of value-based pricing should be applied: the designer should consider innovative product solutions within the new product's targeted category that consumers are likely to perceive worthy of their target prices.

(5) Implementation of DTP

The DTP method is a way to develop and design products that possess customer value worthy of their target prices. Suppose that a comparison of a new product's target price with the reference price for a comparable alternative leads managers to consider that a target price is excessively higher than the reference price (the price that customers would pay for a product or service that they perceive to be similar to the one being offered; Macdivitt and Wilkinson, 2012, p. 115). The price premium of new products or services arises when customers highly values functions and solutions offered by the new product or service. Considering customers' value perception, target pricing may involve the calculation of a new product target price higher than the reference prices, followed by the development and design of new products with functions and solutions consumers deem sufficiently attractive to warrant premium prices. Among the most critical objectives of target pricing is designing new products with excellent benefits that consumers would be willing to buy at a price higher than the reference prices.

According to Macdivitt and Wilkinson (2012, p. 114), the maximum value-based price is calculated as the reference price plus added value. For measuring value added or differentiated customer value in designing new products, Homburg *et al.* (2015) developed a new scale to measure product design along aesthetic, functional, and symbolic dimensions. Aesthetic dimension refers to the perceived appearance and beauty of a product. Functional dimension reveals a product's ability to fulfill its purpose. Symbolic dimension reflects the self-image of consumers about owing the product (Homburg *et al.*, 2015, p. 44). Figure 2.2 shows how a target customer value embraces differentiated value over the standardized value of reference goods. Designing target customer value involves aesthetic, functional, and symbolic dimensions (Homburg *et al.*, 2015). As indicated in Figure 2.2, a price that customers are willing to pay is

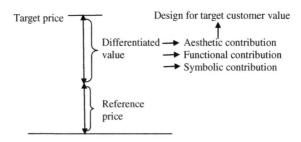

Figure 2.2.   Design for target customer in terms of aesthetic, functional, and symbolic dimensions

Note: Aesthetic, functional, and symbolic dimensions in product design are based on Homburg *et al.* (2015).

calculated as follows: customers' willingness to pay for a new product = its reference price + their monetary benefits from its differentiated aesthetic, functional, and symbolic attributes.

Crucial success factors in implementing target pricing include establishing attractive product differentiation that elicits eagerness to buy, the procurement of new materials and components that can create differentiated products, the development of innovative manufacturing methods dedicated to the production of high-customer-value products, and the creation and cultivation of new marketing channels. Therefore, successful target pricing relies on the high performance of vertical business function, comprised of the development of new products, material and parts fabrication, finished product manufacturing, product marketing, and the distribution of goods. Target pricing-based NPD, thus, requires close cooperation among all supply chain partners, including material makers, components suppliers, assemblers, and marketers. Most importantly, under target pricing-driven NPD, consistent cooperation among supply chain partners is necessary from the early stages of the product life cycle.

3.6. An implementation process for DTP using new sales ratio (NSR)

A useful performance metric for measuring the contribution of new products to business growth is NSR, calculated as the ratio of the current annual sales of new products to total annual sales (Whiteley *et al.*, 1998). The implementation of DTP-driven NPD occurs as follows: (1) new business year's target for NSR is determined, (2) target prices for new products based on the targeted NSR are calculated, and (3) new products that are perceived as worth the targeted prices are designed and developed.

DTP can be successfully implemented by adopting the following two measures. The first requirement is engineering technology that enables the development and design of products worth the premium prices. Second, it is important that consumers understand how to use and their benefits of the new products, so as to promote purchases. Ease of consumer learning that enhances product knowledge is addressed in the next section.

3.7. Effects of learning cost reduction on BET

Switching costs are the expenses incurred when a customer switches to a different provider. Jones *et al.* (2002, pp. 442–443) identified the six types of switching costs customers incur: (1) costs associated with the loss of benefits accrued from the pre-switching partners' trading players; (2) extra costs incurred when post-switching goods are inferior; (3) pre-switching search and evaluation costs; (4) costs incurred in learning how to use a new service; (5) costs associated with the additional learning needed to facilitate customer satisfaction; and (6) non-recoupable sunk costs associated with establishing and maintaining relationships.

Reductions in customers' switching costs contribute to overcoming the barriers to sales increases. This section focuses on how to reduce learning costs required to understand new products or services. To reduce the costs of customers' learning about new products at the early stage of NPD projects, close cooperation between the supply chain partners responsible for marketing and production should be established.

How can customer learning costs be reduced? One solution is establishing own-brand stores wherein visiting customers can gain knowledge about the goods, including how to use them and how they are differentiated from others. Building a customer experience to promote customer learning about the companies also requires offering websites on which visiting customers can obtain product knowledge, thereby reducing customers' learning costs.

How can capital investments for constructing own-brand stores by supply chains be effectively utilized? One solution is as follows. Supply chains can sell products or services and offer product or service information to visiting customers at own-brand stores, and supply chains can learn about consumer needs from those visiting those stores. A reduction in consumers' switching cost is incurred when their change from one supply chain to another contributes to an increase in sales of the latter. This section focuses on a reduction in learning costs in the supply chain.

Products or services in the introduction stage of the product life cycle deliver new functionality to customers. Customers need to understand how to use the new products or services to deliver full satisfaction. Learning costs are cash expenditures required in learning how to use the goods. Learning costs for goods increase along with increases in goods' complexity and novelty. Therefore, supply chains must efficiently offer customers information and experience related to the new products or services to reduce consumers' learning costs, thereby maximizing profits on the new product or service launched.

According to Gallo (2012), to achieve the points stated above, employees are trained to understand customers' needs and acknowledge their questions, resolve their concerns, and help them understand all the benefits of the solutions offered (pp. 97, 102). As shown in Figure 2.1, an efficient reduction in customer learning costs is conducive to increasing the sales revenue from new products or services.

4. Summary

Why do firms enter supply chains? An important motive for establishing an inter-firm supply chain is the enhancement of their own competitive advantage. Outperforming competing supply chains requires strengthened collaborative partnerships among the participants. Put differently, maximization of network capability in supply chains requires a highly integrated partnership. How can supply chains be more integrated? This study examined the effects of motivating the partners to behave in the best interests of the overall supply chain through network-wide communication about how many of its competitive performance goals have been achieved at any point. It also allows partners to ascertain the extent to which the objective of entering the supply chains has been achieved. This study addressed BET as a measure of supply chain competitiveness.

References

Best, R. J. (2009). *Market-Based Management*, Upper Saddle River, NJ: Pearson-Prentice Hall.

Booz, Allen, and Hamilton (1982). *New Product Management for the 1980's*, New York: Booz, Allen & Hamilton, Inc.

Clark, K. B. and Fujimoto, T. (1991). *Product Development Performance: Strategy, Organization, and Management in the World Auto Industry*, Boston, Massachusetts: Harvard Business Review Press.

Cohen, M. A., Eliashberg, J., and Teck-Hua Ho (1996). New Product Development: The Performance and Time-to-Market Tradeoff, *Management Science*, Vol. 42, No. 2, pp. 173–186.

Gallo, C. (2012). *The Apple Experience: Secrets to Building Insanely Great Customer Loyalty*, New York: McGraw-Hill Education.

Hinterhuber, A. (2008). Customer Value-Based Pricing Strategies: Why Companies Resist, *Journal of Business Strategy*, Vol. 29, No. 4, pp. 41–50.

Homburg, C., Schwemmle, M., and Kuehnl, C. (2015). New Product Design: Concept, Measurement, and Consequences, *Journal of Marketing*, Vol. 79, No. 3, pp. 41–56.

House, C. H. and Price, R. L. (1991). The Return Map: Tracking Product Teams, *Harvard Business Review*, January–February, pp. 92–100.

Johne, A. (1994). Listening to the Voice of the Market, *International Marketing Review*, Vol. 11, No. 1, pp. 47–59.

Jones, M. A., Mothersbaugh, D. L., and Beatty, S. E. (2002). Why Customers Stay: Measuring the Underlying Dimensions of Services Switching Costs and Managing Their Differential Strategic Outcomes, *Journal of Business Research*, Vol. 55, No. 6, pp. 441–450.

Krishnan, V., Eppinger, S. D., and Whitney, D. E. (1997). A Model-Based Framework to Overlap Product Development Activities, *Management Science*, Vol. 43, No. 4, pp. 437–451.

Liozu, S. M., Hinterhuber, A., Boland, R., and Perelli, S. (2012). The Conceptualization of Value-Based Pricing in Industrial Firms, *Journal of Revenues and Pricing Management*, Vol. 11, No. 1, pp. 12–34.

Macdivitt, H. and Wilkinson, M. (2012). *Value-Based Pricing: Drive Sales and Boost Your Bottom Line by Creating, Communicating, and Capturing Customer Value*, New York: McGraw-Hill Education.

Makido, T. (1985). Cost Management, in *Production Management*, edited by Ogawa, E., Tokyo: Chuokeizai-Sha, Inc., pp. 125–147 (in Japanese).

Makido, T. (2000). *Japanese-Style Management Accounting and Overseas Transfer*, Kaikei, Vol. 157, No. 3, pp. 1–14 (in Japanese).

Meyer, M. H. and Lehnerd, A. P. (1997). *The Power of Product Platforms*, New York: Simon and Schuster.

Monden, Y. (1995). *Cost Reduction Systems: Target Costing and Kaizen Costing*, Portland, Oregon: Productivity Press.

Ross, D. F. (1998). *Competing Through Supply Chain Management: Creating Market-Winning Strategies Through Supply Chain Partnerships*, New York: Chapman & Hall.

Simatupang, T. M. and Sridharan, R. (2005). An Integrative Framework for Supply Chain Collaboration, *The International Journal of Logistics Management*, Vol. 16, No. 2, pp. 257–274.

Whiteley, R., Parish, T., Dressler, R., and Nicholson, G. (1998). Evaluating R&D Performance: Using the New Sales Ratio, *Research Technology Management*, Vol. 41, No. 5 (September/October), pp. 20–22.

Woodside, A. G., Golfetto, F., and Gibbert, M. (2008). Customer Value: Theory, Research, and Practice, in *Creating and Managing Superior Customer Value*, edited by Woodside, A. G., Golfetto, F., and Gibbert, M., UK: Emerald Group Publishing Limited, pp. 3–25.

Chapter 3

Flexible Supply Chain Management

1. Introduction

Relationship-specific investments in an inter-firm network are the biggest driving force of the network's competitive advantage (Dyer and Singh, 1998). As competition among supply chains becomes harder and fiercer, relationship-specific assets that are dedicated uniquely to a differentiation strategy, to distinguish a supply chain from its competitors, impact on the competitive advantage of the overall supply chain to a greater extent. Nevertheless, it is important to keep in mind that relationship-specific investments, as a competitive weapon, exhibit the characteristic of a high degree of asset specificity. According to Williamson (1991, p. 281), a highly specific asset is related uniquely to one specific objective. Thus, specific assets have limited value for alternative uses.

A key factor of a supply chain's sustainable growth is the development of a trusting relationship among the partners. A partner's assistance in reducing other partners' risks contributes to building trust across the supply chain (Das and Teng, 1998, p. 494). However, supply chain partners are legally separate firms. Moreover, firms do not tend to assume economically unjustified risks solely in others' interest (Das and Teng, 1998, p. 504). Thus, supply chains must reduce the levels of potential risk associated with their entire activities, thereby increasing the effectiveness and efficiency of risk reduction.

The participants in supply chains fulfill the demand for emerging products or services and inherently expose themselves to three types of uncertainty. The first is related to R&D, which poses a challenge with respect to resolving uncertainty. Indeed, uncertainty is intrinsic to innovation. The second is related to the small number of emerging products or services that can achieve dominant position and penetration into markets. The third is related to the heavy investments that the partners in the supply chains for emerging products or services need to make in assets that have a limited range of uses.

This study explores the managerial advantages of a real option-driven multistage capital investment. In this regard, the investment approach seeks to achieve strategic value by flexibly executing risky capital investments (Brealey and Myers, 1996; Panayi and Trigeorgis, 1998). Namely, a real option-based multi-investment can ensure returns from the investment while mitigating the risk inherent in the investment.

2. Impacts of Mitigating Supply Chain Risk on Cooperation among Partners

Risk generically refers to the effects of uncertainty on objectives. In this context, such effects are positive or negative deviations from the expected position (ISO 31000, 2009). The most critical issue for risk management in corporations is that of reducing economic losses caused by uncertainty.

A key factor of a supply chain's sustainable growth is the development of a trusting relationship among the partners. A partner's assistance in reducing other partners' risks contributes to building trust across the supply chain (Das and Teng, 1998, p. 494). However, supply chain partners are legally separate firms. Moreover, firms do no tend to economically unjustified risks solely for the interests of others (Das and Teng, 1998, p. 504). Thus, supply chains must facilitate partners to continually commit their support in the reduction of other partners' risks by reducing the levels of potential risk associated with their entire activities (Minagawa, 2007).

Wu *et al.* (2006) describe six types of supply chain risk. The first refers to internal risk drivers that are mostly controllable by firms. The second refers to internal, partially controllable risk drivers. The third refers to internal uncontrollable risk drivers. The fourth refers to external controllable risk drivers, an example of which is the selection of suppliers.

The fifth refers to external partially controllable risk drivers, an example being shifts in market demand. The sixth refers to external uncontrollable risk drivers, an example of which is a natural disaster (Wu *et al.*, 2006, pp. 352–353).

It is worth noting that it is difficult to forecast the occurrence of external uncontrollable or partially uncontrollable risks. This is because such risks comprise natural disaster occurrences and market demand changes (Wu *et al.*, 2006, p. 353).

Internal risks can be prevented by management resources, comprised of human capital, tangible assets, money, intangible assets, and management control systems. For instance, product quality loss can be prevented by quality improvement by highly professional employees of the company. External risks can be alleviated by management control systems that are adequately matched to the problem that causes the risk. This study deals with the problem of investment irreversibility; the cost of an irreversible investment cannot be recovered once it is committed. The study proposes a real option-assisted management control system that enables flexible capital investment, and the advantage of maximizing the profit while reducing the loss.

The current study considers how supply chains' significant capital investments in emerging markets can be managed. Decisions about capital investments need to allow for external uncontrollable market demand changes. Moreover, achieving returns from capital investments requires the flexibility to absorb market changes that have occurred throughout the investments' entire life cycles. If supply chains can make each partner's management of risky capital investments easier, they can increase supply chain-wide cooperation to support the reduction of other partners' capital investment-driven risks (Minagawa, 2007).

3. Managing Relationship-Specific Investments in Supply Chains

3.1. Managerial challenges of relationship-specific investments in supply chains

Competitive relationship-specific assets are uniquely positioned to solve the problems in a supply chain. Further, such assets in a supply chain are used to solve its problems differently compared with its competitors. Relationship-specific investments require close ties among partners, thereby increasing long-standing integrated inter-firm partnerships. However, relationship-specific investments are riskier because they may have some inherent restrictions with respect to other possible uses. This study examines the advantage of multistage investments as an excellent method to manage relationship-specific investments in supply chains.

Multistage investments can enhance flexibility in management's decision-making when market uncertainty is reduced in the light of emergent information (Panayi and Trigeorgis, 1998, p. 676). A staged investment approach can thus capture strategic options for continuing or discontinuing projects after future cash flow uncertainty has been substantially resolved with latest information. At the time of a decision, if a certain stage of an investment creates an opportunity for profit generation, managers can decide to proceed to increase revenue. However, if at a particular stage of an investment, future growth is shown as impossible, the partners can decide to discontinue the project to avoid further losses.

Supply chain participants must positively make relationship-specific investments. However, if an investment fails to meet a market's demands, the partners in the supply chain need to reduce the consequential losses as much as possible.

3.2. How to strategically and flexibly make a relationship-specific investment

As described in the foregoing analysis, supply chain participants struggle to determine how to make relationship-specific investments in an active manner while simultaneously preventing the failure to recoup the investment costs. To achieve these goals successfully, the application of multistage real options is critically important. This study is not the first to consider a real option approach as a managerial practice relevant to strategic alliances. For example, Das and Teng argue that a multistage real option approach leads to a reduction in risks, thereby enhancing the building of trust (Das and Teng, 1998, p. 504). Gerybadze also emphasizes that a multistage real option approach reduces risk and increases flexibility effectively, leading to enhanced cooperation among firms (Gerybadze, 1994, pp. 105–109).

Hurry *et al.* (1992) showed that investments by Japanese multinational companies in the U.S. high-technology industries were executed based on an "implicit call option" model. The strategic logic underlying the investments reveals flexible, risk-adjusted hedge investments that yield smaller returns but show significant growth. The current study is based on these prior studies. However, they do not discuss how to implement multistage investments. Therefore, this study describes a method by which supply chain participants can undertake staged investments.

How are multistage investment decisions successfully executed? The first theoretical focus in this study is on improving the inadequacy of a conventional investment justification based on discounted cash flow (DCF) to capture the strategic value of a multi-based investment accurately. There are three steps in the traditional DCF-based calculation of an investment's value. The first is to establish the prospective cash flow scenario (Amram and Kulatilaka, 1999, p. 14). The second is to forecast the expected cash flow, period by period. The third is to discount the forecasts in order to present the value at the level of return that a firm could expect to earn on an alternative investment that entails the same risk. The traditional DCF-based investment justification recommends that decision-makers invest if the net present value (NPV) is greater than zero.

What are the recommendations for decision-makers if they rely on the traditional DCF-based method to justify a two-stage investment? A method for a traditional DCF-based investment justification to engage in a two-stage investment is to evaluate the two-stages, namely, the initial trial investment project and the subsequent full-scale investment project, separately and sequentially. Under this method for evaluating two-stage investments, when the initial trial investment project has a negative NPV, the second-stage investment project disappears before it becomes an agenda item for a CEO meeting. Thus, the rejection of the initial investment automatically leads to the rejection of the whole two-stage investment. However, an initial small investment does not tend to generate large net cash inflows.

Another traditional approach to valuing a two-stage investment is to calculate the overall monetary return from the entire investment by regarding it as a stand-alone project. The main drawback of this practice is it does not allow abandoning of the second-stage investment even if market conditions turn unfavorable after starting the initial investment.

Put differently, the traditional DCF-based methods are unable to alter the prospective cash flow scenario established at the outset.

Multistage investments can leverage a time period to access additional information on market conditions thereby enabling the resolution of uncertainty. Thus, a multistage project enables management to alter its future capital investment plans based on new information. Moreover, the effect of such an extension of information is to expand the investment plan's future growth potential and limit its losses (Panayi and Trigeorgis, 1998, p. 676). However, conventional DCF methods cannot appropriately capture the flexibility embedded in multistage investments (Panayi and Trigeorgis, 1998, p. 676). This limitation of conventional DCF methods can be overcome by using real call options. The real call options method applies financial call options theory in order to quantify the value of strategic capital investments.

3.3. How to quantify the value of strategic capital investments using the financial call options theory

A call option is the right to buy stocks by paying a specified exercise price on or before a specified exercise date (Brealey and Myers, 1996, p. 558). The call option holder is not obliged to exercise the call option. This enables call options to be used to hedge risks. If the market price of a stock is lower than the exercise price of the call, the call option holder will not exercise the call option, thereby enabling the holder to limit the losses incurred to the amount paid to acquire the option. However, if the market price of a stock is greater than the exercise price, the call option holder will exercise the call option thus earning a profit.

Black and Scholes (1973) were the first to derive a solution for the equilibrium price of a call option. The valuation of a European call option on an underlying stock is shown below (Black and Scholes, 1973).

$$C = SN(d_1) - Ee^{-rT}N(d_2), \qquad (3.1)$$

where C is the value of a European call option, S is the current price of the underlying stock, $N(d_2)$ is the cumulative standard normal distribution function, E is the exercise price, T is the time to maturity, and r is the risk-free interest rate. Further, $d_2 = d_1 - \sigma\sqrt{T}$, where σ is the volatility of the stock price. Thus

$$d_1 = \frac{\ln\left(\dfrac{S}{E}\right) + \left(r + \dfrac{1}{2}\sigma^2\right)T}{\sigma\sqrt{T}}, \tag{3.2}$$

How are multistage real options valued (Minagawa, 2007)? Inputs for the financial option model are similar to those required to value multistage real options. For example, the present value (PV) of the expected cash flow from the subsequent stages of multistage investments corresponds to the current value of the stock in the financial option. Further, the investment cost for undertaking the subsequent stages of a project is considered the exercise price.

However, the method for calculating the future value of a project's cash flow is controversial. There are very few real assets whose future values are directly quantifiable. If a real asset is not traded in the market, its real option valuation requires the identification of the "twin assets" that carry the same risk as the real option project at the same time as the investment's end of life or termination (Teisberg, 1995, p. 38). An example of the twin assets is the current value of the stock of the firms that have been operating in the identical business category.

Using an example based on Brealey and Myers (1996, pp. 590–592), the remainder of this section illustrates the process of adapting the Black and Scholes formula to the quantification of the flexibility in strategic two-stage investment projects. Currently, we are in the year 2018. At present, the management in corporation X is evaluating a proposed small trial investment in a new product, say α. The trial investment has an expected period of 5 years, from 2018 to 2022, leading to the subsequent creation of the opportunity for full-scale investment in the new product at the second stage. The decision to launch the full-scale new entry of α must be made after 5 years, in 2023. The forecasted net cash inflow and NPV at a 20% hurdle rate of the initial trial investment are as follows: an investment of US$5 million in 2018; investments of US$0.60 million and US$0.50 million in 2019; investments of US$0.65 million and US$0.45 million in 2020; investments of US$0.70 million and $0.41 million in 2021; and investments of US$0.75 and US$0.36 million in 2022.

DCF-based justification for the initial trial investment on a stand-alone basis depends only on the cash flow from the trial investment. Thus, DCF-based assessment gives a negative value of US$32.8 million as the negative total NPV at a 20% hurdle rate, prompting the management to decide not to start the initial trial investment. Unfortunately, this judgment provides the wrong guidance for corporation X. This is because although the trial investment yields not only its own cash flows but also a call option to launch the full-scale entry of the new product, the DCF-based justification does not take the subsequent call option into account. The fact that the subsequent call option results from the trial investment makes the DCF-based calculations' outcome diverge greatly from the real value of the trial investment.

A decision whether or not to invest in the full-scale entry of the new product will be made in 2023, which is the year after the first-stage investment terminates. The decision is grounded on the following assumptions: (1) the investment required is US$50 million (the exercise price); (2) the forecast cash inflow is worth an NPV of US$80 million in 2023 and an NPV of US$32.15 million (US$80 million/$(1.2)^5$) in 2018; (3) the future value of cash flows from the larger, second-stage investment unfolds as corporation X's stock price experiences a standard deviation of 31.5% per year, namely the stock is the "twin security" of the second-stage investment (Trigeorgis and Mason, 1987, p. 15); (4) the annual risk-free rate of interest is 5%; and (5) the hurdle rate is 20%.

Thus, the problem of the justification of the initial trial investment project can be restated as follows: does the monetary value of the opportunity for the full-scale investment created through the initial trial investment exceed the investment outlay of the initial trial investment project? (Kemna, 1993, p. 263) Returning to the above example, calculating the value of a call option (after acquiring the right to undertake the full-scale investment in the second stage) based on Brealey and Myers (1996, pp. 579, 591) results in the following:

$$\text{Standard deviation} \times \sqrt{\text{time}} = 0.315 \times \sqrt{5} = 0.70,$$

$$\frac{\text{Asset value}}{\text{PV}(\text{exercise price})} = \frac{32.15}{50 \Big/ (1.05)^5} = 0.82,$$

$$\frac{\text{Call option}}{\text{Asset value}} = 0.206 \text{ (figure from Appendix Table 6}$$

in Brealey and Myers (1996)),

Call option value $= 0.206 \times 32.15 = 6.6229$.

In sum, the total value of the initial trial investment is its own NPV — US$3.28 million, and the US$6.62 million option added to it.

4. Classification of Multistage Real Options in Supply Chains

This section examines how managerial flexibility embedded in contingent investments can be properly valued. The practices of multistage real options in supply chains may take several forms, including separated (or decentralized) and integrated (or centralized) types. In separated multistage real options in supply chains, individual participants can separately decide either to continue or discontinue their staged investments. Each participant retains the right to have multistage real options. However, integrated staged investments in supply chains emphasize the valuation of the combined return from the multistage real options of the respective participants. Thus, the integrated type determines how a supply chain as a whole should respond to changing markets. In other words, integrated real options lead either to the continuation or discontinuation of multistage investments from the perspective of the whole supply chains. The separated and integrated approaches are examined in depth in the remainder of the section.

4.1. Separated multistage real options

4.1.1. *Partner Reselection*

In a separated (decentralized) multistage real options approach, some partners may not proceed to the next stage of the investment. Thus, partners who decide to proceed to the next stage should find new partners in place of those who did not continue.

In order to facilitate a separated multistage real option, it is important to overcome the uncertainty about whether partners will continue with a project or abandon it. Hence, this inter-firm investment project requires that all partners should know other partners' strategies for the continuation or discontinuation of a project during its execution.

4.1.2. *The Process of Separated Multistage Real Options*

Figure 3.1 shows the entire separated multistage real option process of supply chains. The justification of a multistage investment starts with the projection of the expected cash flow to be earned in each stage of the overall investment. Such projected future cash flow of the respective stages is reconsidered in the context of new information when it emerges.

Suppose that the managers of supply chain firms are attempting to value an investment project that can be regarded as a series of sequential stages. To begin with, the managers must obtain the NPV of the expected future cash flow from the first-stage investment. When evaluating the first-stage investment, the supply chain's participants need to be aware that once the first-stage investment has been undertaken, they can acquire the option either to make the second-stage investment in order to increase revenues or to cease the investment with the aim of limiting the losses. The value of this embedded flexibility must be incorporated in the investment's justification; otherwise, the value of multistage real options is underestimated. Consequently, the strategic NPV of the first-stage investment for each supply chain partner includes both values: the traditional NPV of the expected future cash flow from the first-stage investment and the payoff from real options that enables decisions to be made about whether to continue or discontinue investments in response to market conditions (Trigeorgis, 1998, pp. 121–124).

Let us assume that the strategic NPV of a first-stage investment has shown a positive result; therefore, managers of the supply chain partners have decided to launch the multistage investment. As soon as the first-stage investment starts, managers of the supply chain partners begin to have access to new information that is useful in reconsidering the prior projected strategic NPV of the second-stage investment; namely, the (traditional NPV of the expected cash flow from the second-stage investment + the payoff from the real option for the third-stage investment).

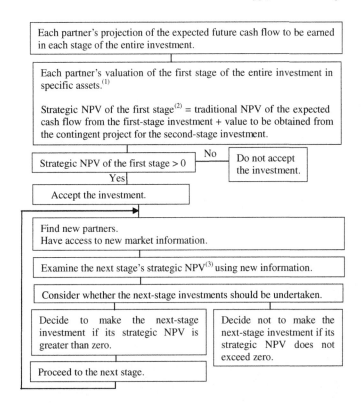

Figure 3.1.   Separated multistage real options in supply chains

Notes:

1. "Specific assets" are based on Williamson (1991).

2. According to Trigeorgis (1998, pp. 121–124), strategic NVP includes both value elements: the traditional NPV of expected cash flow and the real option value of strategic flexibility.

3. The strategic NPV of the following stage investment = the traditional NPV of a given stage + the value to be obtained from the contingent project at the following stage.

This reconsideration of strategic NPV can be implemented by using the information at a given time during the first stage. If the reconsidered and authorized strategic NPV is positive, the supply chain partners decide to proceed to the second stage of the investment.

It should be noted that during the first stage, the supply chain needs to facilitate communication regarding partners' continuation or discontinuation in the investment project. If some partners decide not to invest in the second stage of the project, those that remain and wish to invest need to find new partners. Immediately after launching the second stage, partners' managers begin to have access to new information. This information can help to resolve uncertainty about the possibility of generating positive cash flows in the third stage.

Thus, processes for making a multistage real option analysis subsequent to the second stage begin with having access to new information that may contribute to altering the staged investment strategy. This access is followed by a reexamination of the prior projected strategic NPV of a given stage using the new information. Finally, a decision is made to continue or stop the investment in accordance with the authorized strategic NPV.

4.2. Integrated multistage real options in supply chains

4.2.1. *The Process of Integrated Multistage Real Options*

This process values the combined return of each partner's multistage investment (see Figure 3.2). Such an approach, based on the combined return, leads to an overall supply chain strategy that addresses how supply chains as a whole should respond to changing markets. In this regard, integrated multistage real options in supply chains result in a solution to enable the entire supply chain to continue or discontinue staged investments. When applying this valuation, it is important to share evenly the overall returns yielded or the total losses suffered across the supply chain among the partners.

Figure 3.2 shows that if the combined strategic NPV of a first-stage investment indicates a positive result, the supply chain decides to launch a multistage investment. Immediately after the first-stage investment starts, managers of the supply chain partners begin to have access to new information that is useful for reconsidering the previously projected NPV of the second-stage investment, namely, the traditional NPV of the expected cash flow from the second-stage investment + the payoff from the real option for the third-stage investment. This reconsideration of strategic NPV is made using the information available at a given time

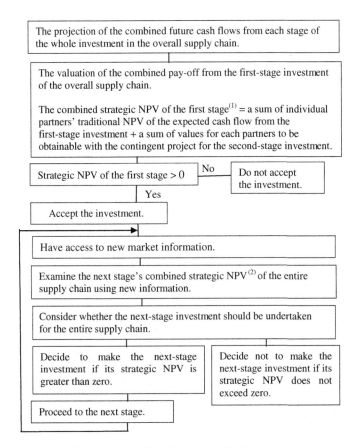

Figure 3.2. Integrated multistage real options in supply chain

Notes:

1. According to Trigeorgis (1998, pp. 121–124), strategic NVP includes both value elements: the traditional NPV of expected cash flows and the real option value of strategic flexibility.

2. The strategic NPV of the following stage investment = a given stage's traditional NPV + value to be obtainable with the contingent project for the following stage.

during the first stage. If the finally authorized combined strategic NPV is positive, the supply chain partners decide to proceed to the second stage of the investment.

After the partners invest capital in the second stage of the project, they begin to have access to relevant information for resolving uncertainty related to the possibility of the third stage generating a positive cash flow.

To undertake a multistage real option analysis subsequent to the second stage, partners need information that may contribute to altering the staged investment strategy. The partners can then reexamine the prior projected strategic NPV of a given stage using the new information and finally arrive at a decision about whether or not to continue the investment in accordance with the authorized combined strategic NPV.

4.2.2. *Incentive Scheme*

To implement integrated multistage real options successfully, supply chains must motivate all partners to invest capital in order to increase their joint profits. A useful practice is the allocation of the supply chain's joint profit to the partners in accordance with their costs. This profit sharing in a supply chain allows partners to recognize that they can increase their profits by making capital investments toward increasing the supply chain's overall profit. Partners can indeed increase their shares of the joint profit by making capital investments to increase the supply chain's joint profit. Furthermore, the allocation of the supply chain's joint profit among the partners, based on their costs, helps them recover their investments. This, in turn, promotes capital investments throughout the chain.

5. Conclusions

This study explored ways to implement the real-option-initiated multistage investment and the strategic advantages of the investment approach. Further, the study showed the impact of changing partners on facilitating cooperative relationship-specific capital investments across supply chains.

References

Amram, M. and Kulatilaka, N. (1999). *Real Options: Managing Strategic Investment in an Uncertain World*, Boston: Harvard Business School Press.

Black, F. and Scholes, M. (1973). The Pricing of Options and Corporate Liabilities, *Journal of Political Economy*, Vol. 81, No. 3, pp. 637–654.

Brealey, R. A. and Myers, S. C. (1996). *Principles of Corporate Finance* (5th Edition), New York: McGraw-Hill.

Das, T. K. and Teng, B. S. (1998). Between Trust and Control: Developing Confidence in Partner Cooperation in Alliances, *Academy of Management Review*, Vol. 23, No. 3, pp. 491–512.

Dyer, J. H. and Singh, H. (1998). The Relational Review: Cooperative Strategy and Sources of Inter-organizational Competitive Advantage, *The Academy of Management Review*, Vol. 23, No. 4, pp. 660–679.

Gerybadze, A. (1994). *Strategic Alliances and Process Redesign: Effective Management and Restructuring of Cooperative Projects and Networks*, Berlin: Walter de Gruyter.

Hurry, H., Miller, A. T., and Bowman, E. H. (1992). Call on High-Technology: Japanese Exploration of Venture Capital Investments in the United States, *Strategy Management Journal*, Vol. 13, No. 2, pp. 85–101.

ISO (International Organization for Standardization) (2009). *ISO 31000 Risk Management — Principles and Guidelines*, Geneva: International Organization for Standardization.

Kemna, A. G. Z. (1993). Case Studies on Real Options, *Financial Management*, Autumn, pp. 259–270.

Minagawa, Y. (2007). How Can Supply Chain Risks Be Reduced by Mutual Cooperation among Partners–Application of Real Options and Throughput Accounting, in *Japanese Management Accounting Today*, edited by Monden, Y., Kosuga, M., Nagasaka, Y., Hiraoka, S., and Hoshi, N., Singapore: World Scientific Publishing Co., pp. 177–192.

Panayi, S. and Trigeorgis, L. (1998). Multi-Stage Real Options: The Cases of Information Technology Infrastructure and International Bank Expansion, *The Quarterly Review of Economics and Finance*, Vol. 38, No. 3, Special Issue, pp. 675–692.

Teisberg, E. O. (1995). Methods for Evaluating Capital Investment Decisions under Uncertainty, in *Real Options in Capital Investment: Models, Strategies, and Applications*, edited by Trigeorgis, L., Santa Barbara: Praeger, pp. 31–45.

Trigeorgis, E. O. (1998). *Real Options: Managing Flexibility and Strategy in Resource Allocation*, Cambridge, MA: The MIT Press.

Trigeorgis, L. and Mason, S. (1987). Valuing Managerial Flexibility, *Midland Corporate Finance Journal*, Spring, pp. 14–21.

Williamson, O. E. (1991). Comparative Economic Organization: The Analysis of Discrete Structural Alternatives, *Administrative Science Quarterly*, Vol. 36, No. 2, pp. 269–296.

Wu, T., Blackhurst, J., and Chidambaram, V. (2006). A Model for Inbound Supply Chain Risk Analysis, *Computers in Industry*, Vol. 57, No. 4, pp. 350–365.

Chapter 4

Supply Chain Balanced Scorecard for Customer Satisfaction

1. Introduction

Sales promotion significantly and positively affects firms' financial performance. The sales growth of a firm depends largely on its ability to satisfy customer needs through its products or services. For this purpose, supply chains must increase customer satisfaction to boost their sales of the finished products. This can be achieved by formulating an appropriate strategy for the fulfillment of customer needs and determining how to quantify customer satisfaction. The study examines the advantages of a balanced scorecard-assisted managerial planning aimed at increasing customer satisfaction in the supply chain.

The rest of the chapter is organized as follows. The next section studies what customer satisfaction is, through a review of related literature. Then, the study goes on to examine how it can be increased. Furthermore, the impacts of the balanced scorecard approach on enhancing customer value in a supply chain are revealed in the study.

2. Related Literature Review

2.1. Strategy and the balanced scorecard

2.1.1. *Strategy*

According to Simons (2000, p. 16), corporate strategy defines a scenario that a firm exploits to maximize the value of the resources it controls. The comprehensive agendas in the formulation of a corporate strategy involve what products or services to offer, where to serve, what custom segment to target, and how to differentiate from competitors. Furthermore, the implementation of the business and product or service planning also involves decisions on optimal management of human capital and corporate resources.

According to Hambrick and Fredrickson (2001), the issues to address in formulating strategies are what business and where to compete in, how to enter the target business, how to gain competitive advantages, by when and how to reach business goals, and how to obtain returns.

Firms' sustainable competitive advantages that can distinguish them from their competitors include highly differentiated functions and benefits that customers can obtain through products or services, products or services at an affordable price, conformity to specifications, shorter delivery time, excellent after-sales service, and easily accessible distribution channel, and entrenched brand loyalty (Makido *et al.*, 1998).

Customers in growing markets assign the highest value to the functional uniqueness and novelty of products or services. As the products or services pass into the maturity stage of their life cycle processes, it becomes impossible or more difficult to create a new product or service. Hence, the key success factors for competitiveness during the maturity stage consist of price, quick delivery, after-sales service, and distribution channels. This study focuses on how to promote a new product or service, which is often a strategic issue in the start-up stage of the product life cycle.

2.1.2. *Balanced Scorecard*

According to Kaplan and Norton (1992), the balanced scorecard delineates how to achieve the target profit as an ultimate financial outcome for company success from four perspectives: financial, customer, internal process, and learning and growth (Kaplan and Norton, 1992).

From Kaplan and Norton (1992), the strategic themes on which each perspective of the balanced scorecard sheds light are as follows: the financial perspective, internal and external, conveys the business performance to be attained by implementing various strategies. Firms are unable to earn profit without customer satisfaction. Consequently, the customer perspective articulates how to create customer value. Customer satisfaction can be increased through corporate activities that leverage human capital and corporate resources. Therefore, corporates should create customer-centric, value-added activities and execute them effectively and efficiently. The internal process perspective creates activities that can improve customer value and their performance metrics. The learning and growth perspective examines acquiring intangible assets dedicated to implementing strategies.

According to Kaplan and Norton (2004, p. 55), strategy-driven intangible assets include human capital; the skills, talent, and knowledge that a company's employees possess; the company's information capital; databases, information systems, networks, technology infrastructure, and organization capital; the company's culture and its leadership; the extent to which its people identify themselves with its strategic goals; and employees' ability to share knowledge. The achievement of strategic scenarios entails a balanced scorecard that tells what activities to perform, how to perform them, and the activities' respective performance targets.

The balanced scorecard focuses on a strategy's cause-and-effect relationships, namely vertical and horizontal. The vertical cause-and-effect relationship is found within the chain of the four perspectives. The financial perspective presents the objectives for profit performance. Solutions from the customer perspective involve how to satisfy customers to achieve the financial targets. An analysis from the internal process perspective reveals the effective internal processes to increase customer satisfaction. The perspective of learning and growth indicates how to acquire the intangible capital needed to implement strategies.

The horizontal cause-and-effect relationship is found among the key performance indicators of strategic objectives for individual perspectives. They are the leading and lagging indicators in the balanced scorecard. Leading indicators are objectives in terms of operational performance. Continuous achievement of leading indicators leads to attainment of goals in terms of performance outcomes (Kaplan and Norton, 2001, pp. 76–77).

2.2. Balanced scorecard for supply chain management

There are two types of balanced scorecards for supply chain management. In the first type, each participant in a supply chain formulates its balanced scorecard (Park *et al.*, 2005). The second type is the overall balanced scorecard for the entire supply chain through collaborative partnerships (Zimmermann, 2002).

Park *et al.* (2005) set up a framework for designing the balanced supply chain scorecard. The balanced scorecard of each participant includes the external business process perspective which aims at measuring how well the managerial activities of all participants were integrated into the profitability of the supply chain. The external business process perspective specifically measures the degree of improvement in sourcing leadership, and collaboration with partners, as well as the extent of improvement in purchase order transaction efficiency (Park *et al.*, 2005, p. 342). According to Park *et al.* (2005, p. 342), measures for improving collaboration with partners include order information sharing, inventory information sharing, forecast information sharing, and trust among partners. Their research shows that information sharing among participants in a supply chain substantially enhances trust building in the supply chain.

Zimmermann (2002) explores the advantages of an inter-enterprise supply chain balanced scorecard to implement a joint supply chain strategy.

2.3. Customer satisfaction

2.3.1. *Customer Perspective of the Balanced Scorecard*

Kaplan and Norton (1996) state that the customer perspective of the balanced scorecard identifies those attributes that companies must include in their products or services to satisfy customer needs. The attributes are classified into three categories. The first category comprises functionality, price, and quality. The second category is the image and reputation of product/service. A reputable image enables customers to identify and differentiate the product or service from their competitors. The third category is customer relations that include quick delivery of goods and overall customer experience in purchasing from the company (Kaplan and Norton, 1996, pp. 61–62).

The customer satisfaction perspective of the balanced scorecard leads to strategies that differentiate the firm from its competitors by selling the most attractive new product or service at the most reasonable price. In addition, it is important to provide customer service that can potentially bring about long-standing customer loyalty. According to Womack and Jones (2005), the basic requirements of a highly valued customer service are as follows: (1) solving any problems faced by consumers completely, (2) prompting the valuable utilization of consumer time, (3) providing the right customers with the right items in the right stores exactly at the right time, (4) continually adding new value to goods (pp. 61–67).

2.3.2. *Customer Relationship Management Using the Balanced Scorecard*

Kim *et al.* (2003) established a model for enhancing customer relationship using the balanced scorecard. They show a customer-centric balanced scorecard consisting of the following four perspectives. The first perspective refers to customer value and shows how to enhance customer loyalty and profit. The second perspective refers to customer satisfaction and shows which strategies can increase the level of satisfaction delivered by products or services. The third perspective refers to customer interaction that indicates how to improve operational effectiveness and customer service. The fourth perspective refers to customer knowledge that explores strategies for understanding customers and analyzing customer information (Kim *et al.*, 2003, p. 10).

2.3.3. *Customers Seek Transition as Time Proceeds*

A sequence of customer activities consists of three phases: prepurchase, at purchase, and post-purchase (Sawhney, 2006, p. 372). The sort of service a customer wants varies for each phase in the customer activity process. Upon identifying the purchase needs, the customer decides what product or service to buy during the prepurchase stage. For making a successful purchase decision, customers first need certain information, such as what products or services are available, where can they be bought, and what traits the alternative products or services possess (Sawhney, 2006, p. 372).

At the purchase stage, customers want to enjoy the benefits of the products or services immediately after buying them. Moving to the post-purchase phase, the primary issue regarding how to increase customer satisfaction changes into developing a scheme to continually deliver benefits and living up to customers' expectations. Customers expect the following services: learning the methods to become more knowledgeable about how to effectively use the purchased goods, quickly solving problems that occur when using the goods, and upgrading the benefits derived from the goods (Sawhney, 2006, p. 372).

3. Identifying Drivers of Customer Satisfaction from the Goods Life Cycle Perspective

Customer satisfaction as seen from the product life cycle perspective means only new products or services that succeeded in meeting customer satisfaction can proceed to the next stage. Therefore, the sustainable growth of firms entails launching successful products or services. Hence, this study explores how to raise customer satisfaction during the start-up stage of the products or services life cycle.

One of the most important success factors for new product introduction is the communication of product or service knowledge to the customer, which can arouse his/her eagerness to purchase. The remainder of this section considers the performance indicators and actions for enhancing customer satisfaction through introduction and knowledge provision for a new product or service.

One performance indicator for new product introductions is new product sales ratio, that is, the ratio of the current annual sales of new products to total annual sales (Whitley *et al.*, 1998). Setting the target of the new product sales ratio in supply chains can motivate the partners to work together toward developing and supplying new end products. This is because participating firms along the supply chain typically require the successful supply of new end products to boost their profits. An improved new sales ratio in a supply chain positively influences the profitability of all its participants.

A useful way for formulating profitable new products or services to be developed is the target-pricing approach. This approach requires supply chain participants including marketers, component suppliers, finished product makers, and distributors to make use of each other's expertise by sharing knowledge.

The target-pricing-based new product development in the supply chain entails overall profit planning and product portfolio analysis. These aspects are useful in calculating the target return on sales for new products. Supply chains then determine the target price for new products in accordance with their targeted returns on sales. Lastly, the target-pricing approach allows a product that can realize the target price in the market to be designed. The aim of target pricing is to create an appropriate concept and design for new goods for which customers are willing to pay the target price.

A valuable practice that can promote the provision of product or service knowledge to customers is to invest and establish retail stores devoted to selling the supply chains' finished products. The retail stores run by a supply chain are suitable places where visitors can learn by experience. These customers can become acquainted with the supply chain's products or services. They can also gain a better understanding about the supply chain's products or services through their communication with the store staff. They can learn how to use products or services more effectively as well as the differentiated value of products or services. Moreover, customers can convey their expectations for the upcoming new products or services to the companies. Such learning-driven customer satisfaction at the retailing stores can drive customers to the supply chains' products or services.

Besides offering product information to customers at brick-and-mortar shops, that is, retail stores with a physical building, supply chains need to invest in developing and leveraging online strategic marketing systems to communicate with customers.

4. Successful New Product Launches and Product/Service Knowledge Provision

The common success factor for new product introduction and product or service knowledge provision is the integration of supply chain participants' expertise into the supply chain's performance. This is explained as follows.

4.1. Effects of sharing expertise on new product development among participants in the supply chains

The first step in the new product development process is concept development for the new product or service. At this stage, planners who are responsible for creating new product concepts need to integrate market and technology knowledge into such concepts (Fujimoto, 1997, p. 29). Furthermore, the early establishment of higher customer-value-centric product or service concepts in the process of new product or service development can contribute to the successful creation of a new product or service. For an enhanced performance of new product or service development, it is essential to address various issues, including what products or services consumers really want, and how firms should create and supply those products or services. Much of the market and technology know-how required to solve the problems associated with new product or service development is obtained by individual firms responsible for the business operations at the various stages of the supply chain process. Therefore, successful creation and supply of new products or services is possible by effectively integrating the different competences of the supply chain partners into products or services that can satisfy consumer wants.

Sobek *et al.* (1999) studied Toyota's principles of set-based concurrent engineering. Under the set-based design approach, a design team first develops a broader set of design solution alternatives by making full use of other members' expertise. They then gradually eliminate weaker solutions according to the design constraint conditions by taking advantage of additional information from the customer and other members, thereby finally finding the best solutions (Sobek *et al.*, 1999, p. 70). The design team is composed of parts suppliers, end product production companies, and marketers in a supply chain.

By contrast, traditional design practices tend to quickly find a promising solution, and then continually modify the solution until it meets the design objective. The subsequent iteration to refine can be time-consuming (Sobek *et al.*, 1999, p. 68). By integrating the supply chain participants, set-based design seeks to avoid multiple iterations to reach the best solution.

4.2. Fostering an experienced and knowledgeable consumer

The creation of a customer value-centric design concept for a new product or service entails integration of the expertise of participants in the new product development. Creating and offering sales promotion information that can prompt customers to buy goods requires cooperation among the participants.

According to Hinterhuber's study on the value-based pricing in firms (2008), ensuring that customers understand the attractiveness of products or services contributes to growth in sales. Moreover, communication of information can deepen the ties between firms and customers. The interactions with customers can help a firm receive feedback about their product or service needs.

Effective coordination of supply chain participants' expertise is considerably conducive to creating product or service information (and knowledge) that can arouse customers' intention to purchase. A motivation for supply chain participants to cooperate fully to provide product or service information to customers is the supply chain-wide sharing of information concerning market needs for new products. An effective practice for capturing customers' needs accurately is to establish real retail stores, where the employees can interact face-to-face with the visiting customers. Therefore, it is important that all supply chain participants actively engage in the retail store operations. The financial commitment of participants to the retail store business contributes toward strengthening their responsibilities for the retail store operation including the provision of product or service knowledge, thereby raising their incentive to leverage customer feedback information across the supply chain.

5. Customer Satisfaction Improvement Using the Balanced Scorecard for Supply Chain Management

The malfunctioning of a supply chain is caused by inappropriate measurement of performance, outdated policies, asymmetric information, and incentive misalignment (Simatupang and Sridharan, 2002). Supply chains must eliminate these conflict-triggering factors. Otherwise, they will not be able to achieve close cooperation among the participants. The balanced scorecard for supply chain management aims at motivating participating firms to work together toward increasing the supply chain's sustainable growth and overall profit. Under the balanced scorecard-initiated supply chain coordination, the participants cooperate to formulate a strategic plan. While the participating firms get involved in formulating the balanced scorecard, they should be aware of the role they are expected to play in dedicating themselves toward implementing the supply chain strategy.

The remainder of the section examines how planning using a balanced scorecard approach can increase customer satisfaction in a supply chain.

5.1. Financial perspective

Return on total assets (ROA) is a primary profitability metric.

ROA can be broken down into the following components:

$$\text{ROA} = (\text{net income} / \text{net sales}) \times (\text{net sales} / \text{total assets})$$
$$= \text{net profit margin} \times \text{total asset turnover}$$

For improving ROA, it is important to increase the net profit margin and total asset turnover simultaneously. The best practices for the highest net profit margin include the creation of innovative products that can drive customers' preference and willingness to pay high prices. However, the creation of new products or services entails high costs. Nevertheless, if the uniqueness and novelty of the new product or service can convince the customers to agree to a price increase greater than the increased costs of the new product or service, then such offerings can produce greater net profit margin. In other words, if an increase in revenue due to enhanced prices that customers are willing to pay in exchange for buying attractive goods is more than the enhanced cost of the goods, a higher net profit margin can be generated.

Notably, increasing the ROA requires the higher sales. To implement this successfully, firms must make the consumer fully understand a product or service's novelty and justification for the high price (Hinterhuber, 2008).

By contrast, as products or services mature and standardize in their life cycle, firms cannot create new goods. Therefore, a key success factor for firms' survival is cost savings. The most important strategic goal is increased total asset turnover. The management measures to improve the total asset turnover involve the elimination of non-value-added activities. The first step in identifying non-value-added activities is calculating the cost of the resources used in each activity — activity-based cost — to ascertain those activities that involve excessive costs.

5.2. Customer perspective

An important driver of customer satisfaction in new products or services is the acceptance of functionality excellence and benefit differentiated from the competitors. Therefore, the competitive advantage for new products or services relies substantially on customers' reputation, backed up by the highest functionality presently available for them.

For mature and standardized products or services, an effective strategy for motivating customers to buy is to make them available when needed at low cost. Consequently, customer satisfaction performance metrics for standardized products or services include quick delivery and low stock-out ratio.

The above performance indicators for the two product types are summarized as follows:

Type of product/service	Lag indicators	Lead indicators
Standardized products or services	Sales growth	Decreasing stock-out and on-time delivery
New products or services	Sales growth	Customer's high evaluation of new products' or services' newness

5.3. Supply chain system perspective

This perspective is based on the value system in Porter's study (1985). The value system consists of different customer value-creating activities conducted by participants in the supply chain.

The supply chain system perspective offers valuable practices for the establishment of partnerships aimed at working together to cope with the changing market demands. Strategic themes addressed from this perspective include effectively integrating supply chain participants' knowledge and expertise into successful new product creation and reducing the supply chain lead time between placing an order and the actual delivery.

From the supply chain system perspective, strategic themes related to customer satisfaction are introduction of new products or services and their quick supply. These performance indicators are explained below:

(1) **Performance indicators for new product launches**

All participants in the supply chain are required to work collaboratively to conduct consumer research on a regular basis. A more effective consumer research practice is the cooperative analyses of information on new products or services and market needs, collected from the visiting customers of supply chains' captive retail stores.

Frequent meetings among supply chain participants to carry out the market research, a leading indicator, lead to an enhanced new product sales ratio. The ratio is a lagging indicator.

(2) **Performance indicators for the quick supply of products or services**

Regular and timely sharing of information about customer orders and demand among all participants in a supply chain is helpful in the synchronization of response to changing markets along the supply chain. This leading indicator results in improved stock-out.

5.4. Growth and learning perspective

The most important strategic goal from the perspective of growth and learning is the enhanced knowledge sharing among the supply chain partners. This study focuses on the significance of sharing information about new product needs and market demand among the participants. This would then drive improvement in the supply chain performance in new product launches and quick delivery.

A facilitating factor for information sharing across the supply chain is incentive alignment among the partners, which aims at inducing the partners to realize that increasing the supply chain's joint profit leads to boosting their own profits. An effective means to integrate the participants' business operational efforts with the supply chain's joint profit is the allocation of the supply chain's joint profit among all the participants. This study shows the contribution of a supply chain's joint profit allocation among the partners to increasing knowledge sharing along the supply chain. Supply chain-wide sharing of information on new product needs and market demand can facilitate introduction and quick delivery of new products or services to satisfy those needs.

6. Concluding Remarks

The strategic agendas of the four perspectives in the supply chain balanced scorecard for customer value improvement examined in the study are summarized in Figure 4.1.

Net profit margins can be improved by the following approach. Cost-based allocation of supply chains' joint profit among partners can

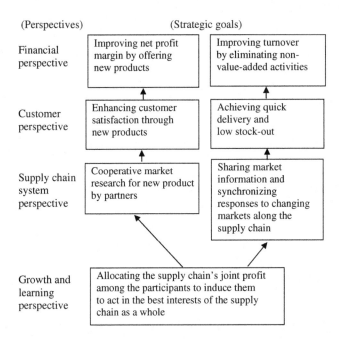

Figure 4.1.   Customer satisfaction management using the balanced scorecard

promote supply chain-wide collaborative market research for new product development. Partnership-based participatory marketing research contributes to successful new product development.

A successful path for achieving turnover improvement by eliminating non-value activities is as follows: allocation of supply chains' joint profit can motivate partners to share market information, thereby accelerating responses to market changes.

References

Fujimoto, T. (1997). *Evolution of Production System*, Tokyo: Yuhikaku (in Japanese).

Hambrick, D. C. and Fredrickson, J. W. (2001). Are You Sure Have a Strategy? *The Academy of Management Executive*, Vol. 15, No. 4, pp. 48–59.

Hinterhuber, A. (2008). Customer Value-Based Pricing Strategies: Why Companies Resist, *Journal of Business Strategy*, Vol. 29, No. 4, pp. 41–50.

Kaplan, R. S. and Norton, D. P. (1992). The Balanced Scorecard: Measures that Drive Performance, *Harvard Business Review*, January–February, pp. 71–79.

Kaplan, R. S. and Norton, D. P. (1996). Linking the Balanced Scorecard to Strategy, *California Management Review*, Vol. 39, No. 1, pp. 53–79.

Kaplan, R. S. and Norton, D. P. (2001). *The Strategy-Focused Organization: How Balanced Scorecard Companies Thrive in the New Business Environment*, Boston: Harvard Business School Press.

Kaplan, R. S. and Norton, D. P. (2004). Measuring the Strategic Readiness of Intangible Assets, *Harvard Business Review*, February, pp. 52–63.

Kim, J., Suh, E., and Hwang, H. (2003). A Model for Evaluating the Effectiveness of CRM Using the Balanced Scorecard, *Journal of Interactive Marketing*, Vol. 17, No. 2, pp. 5–19.

Makido, T., Minagawa, Y., and Kimura, S. (1998). *Japanese Firms' Competitiveness and Managerial Techniques and Practices*, Economic Research No. 108, Economic Research Center, School of Economics Nagoya University (in Japanese).

Park, J. H., Lee, J. K., and Yoo, J. S. (2005). A Framework for Designing the Balanced Supply Chain Scorecard, *European Journal of Information Systems*, Vol. 14, No. 4, pp. 335–346.

Porter, M. E. (1985). *Competitive Advantage: Creating and Sustaining Superior Performance*, New York: Free Press.

Sawhney, M. (2006). Going Beyond the Product: Defining, Designing, and Delivering Customer Solutions, in *The Service-Dominant Logic of*

Marketing: Dialog, Debate, and Direction, edited by Lusch, R. F. and Vargo, S. L., USA: M.E. Shape Inc., New York City, pp. 365–380.

Simatupang, T. M. and Sridharan, R. (2002). The Collaborative Supply Chain, *The International Journal of Logistics Management*, Vol. 13, No. 1, pp. 15–30.

Simons, R. (2000). *Performance Measurement and Control Systems for Implementing Strategy*, New York: Prentice Hall.

Sobek II, D. K., Ward, A. C., and Liker, J. K. (1999). Toyota's Principles of Set-Based Concurrent Engineering, *Sloan Management Review*, Vol. 40, No. 2, pp. 67–83.

Whitley, R., Parish, T., Dressler, R., and Nicholson, G. (1998). R&D Metrics: Evaluating R&D Performance Using the New Sales Ratio, *Research Technology Management*, Vol. 41, No. 5, pp. 20–22.

Womack, J. P. and Jones, D. T. (2005). Lean Consumption, *Harvard Business Review*, Vol. 83, No. 3, pp. 58–68.

Zimmermann, K. (2002). Using the Balanced Scorecard for Interorganizational Performance Management of Supply Chain — A Case Study, in *Cost Management in Supply Chains*, edited by Seuring, S. and Goldbach, M., Heidelberg: Physica-Verlag, pp. 363–380.

Chapter 5

Fabless Supply Chains Management

1. Introduction

Vertical integration is a business model wherein one firm is completely responsible for executing a whole range of functional business operations from new product development to the production and distribution of consumer products. A vertically integrated firm that engages itself in the entire process of generating value for customers can ultimately control the value chain.

However, because a vertically integrated firm is responsible for upstream, midstream, and downstream business functions; it must face the challenge of increased capital requirements. This study addresses capital investments in new product development. New products fall in the growth stage of the technology life cycle, where there is huge scope for product innovation. Product innovation on the supply side can further increase market demand for new products. Hence, products in the growth stage of technology life cycle can facilitate product technology breakthroughs. At the same time, markets for growth-stage products regularly generate among consumers an expectation for a continuous flow of new products, making it impossible for firms to survive unless they keep releasing new products. This competitive environment inevitably mandates increase in capital investment.

Therefore, firms that serve growing product markets face the challenge of raising sufficient funds, to survive the product innovation races. Implementing a fabless supply chain strategy is one way of fulfilling the enhanced capital requirements needed for R&D. Popular new technology products are indicative of the spurt in the growth cycle of technological development; this cycle holds huge potential for product innovation. Increased emphasis on product innovation on the supply side has further stimulated market demand for new products. Consequently, industries that supply popular new products enforce competition rules, which ensure that supply chain companies can increase profits only if they constantly innovate new products. Surviving profitably in such a competitive environment mandates that companies increase their capital investment. The ability to deliver new products at lowest possible costs is the most important competitive advantage for supply chains in growing product markets. A fabless business strategy enables speedier acquisition of new products, thereby benefiting consumers. Fabless firms (i.e., firms without fabrication facilities) utilize their time and resources for the development and marketing of innovative products, and outsource manufacturing to electronics manufacturing service (EMS) providers. Likewise, EMS providers too, must invest in the development of new products and production techniques. Innovation in the EMS providers enables them to satisfy the requirements of fabless firms, and also to launch their new businesses. Since the participants in a fabless supply chain are independent legal entities, they are free to act according to their own interests. To ensure cooperation between firms in fabless supply chains, participants need to address and curb the temptation of opportunistic behavior. Opportunistic behavior refers to "self-interest seeking with guile" (Williamson, 1985, p. 47). The problem of opportunism arises mainly due to asymmetric information (Perloff, 2008, p. 637).

Asanuma's studies on supplier–buyer relationships in the Japanese automobile industry defined two types of part suppliers: "drawing supplied" suppliers that manufacture parts according to the drawings supplied by core firms, and "drawing approved" suppliers that manufacture parts as per drawings created by themselves and approved by core firms. The study principally considers EMS providers that are categorized as "drawing supplied" suppliers (Asanuma, 1988). The analytical study detailed below has been conducted based on a research model wherein a fabless company's competitive edge stems mainly from developing innovative goods in cooperation with its EMS providers, who utilize drawings supplied by the fabless company to fabricate high-powered goods. The next chapter examines how to integrate both types of supply chains: supply chains that include drawing-supplied suppliers and supply chains that include drawing-approved suppliers.

Opportunistic behavior is categorized into two types: adverse selection and moral hazard (Perloff, 2008, p. 637). Adverse selection refers to the market failure that can occur when players in the markets have asymmetric information (Perloff, 2008, p. 637). In such a market, better-informed market players may exploit the lesser-informed ones. When lesser-informed market players become aware of the well-informed players' incentives to exploit them, they can underestimate the value of the traded goods, and thereby refrain from entering into transactions with well-informed market players. Therefore, asymmetric information results in market failure by preventing desirable transactions. Moral hazard relates to the problem of inducing market players to act in good faith, when their actions cannot be observed directly and, therefore, contracted upon (Holmström, 1982, p. 324).

This study sheds light on the allocation of a supply chain's joint profit among the partners as a valuable administrative practice for enhancing cooperation in a fabless supply chain. The main aim of the study is to explore the most appropriate rules that can be used in distributing the supply chain's joint profit among its members, and understanding how profit sharing among participants in a supply chain impacts the integration of the supply chain.

2. A Core Driver of the Competitive Advantage of Fabless Supply Chains

To explore the essential competitive advantage of fabless supply chains, this section considers a supply chain, consisting of firms in charge of R&D (Research and Development), and, EMS providers. The R&D firm's achievement of sustainable growth relies largely on, whether it can establish an inter-firm partnership with high-powered EMS providers. Let us consider that an R&D firm succeeds in developing and designing high-quality new products; however, unless the R&D firm establishes close ties with capable EMS providers, it cannot transform its new product drawings into finished goods.

Just as R&D firms cannot increase profit without partnering with competent EMS providers, EMS providers too cannot boost profits, without allying with R&D firms that have enhanced technological capabilities.

3. Incentive-Alignment-Driven Cooperation Enhancement in Fabless Supply Chains

3.1. Facilitating cooperation between fabless firms and EMS providers

An approach to supply chain integration is power-centric coercion, in which the most powerful focal firms rely on their bargaining power to extract favorable behavior from participants with lesser bargaining power. Opinions are divided on the merits and demerits of supply chain integration that is driven by power-centric coercion. This study explores the source of power, and how this power influences the integration of all participants in an inter-firm networks, linked by collaborative process, according to the work of Maloni and Benton (2000).

Maloni and Benton (2000, p. 54) showed the following six types of inter-firm power: first, focal firms offer pecuniary rewards and the promise of additional business that is accompanied by additional pecuniary rewards for the partners. This has a positive influence on the integration of inter-firm networks. Second, partners can establish rules regarding the imposition of penalties, to dissuade engagement in opportunistic behavior, thereby, ultimately generating inter-firm power. Third, when the supply chain offers participants access to knowledge and skills the latter desire, it increases their dependence on the supply chain. Fourth, if firms highly value being part of certain supply chains, they desire association with those supply chains. Fifth, creating parent-subsidiary relationships can lead to an effective supply chain management. Sixth, the focal firms of supply chains rely on their judiciary right to influence participants in order to promote supply chain integration.

This study extracts three primal types of inter-firm power found in supply chains, as established by Maloni and Benton (2000). The first is coercive power, wherein the source (i.e., the most powerful firms) copes with the opportunistic behavior of the targets (i.e., other participants) by imposing penalties. The second is incentive alignment, wherein the source awards pecuniary rewards, desired knowledge, and skills to the targets, thereby motivating them to behave in the interest of the entire supply chain. The third is contract compliance, wherein the source enters into a contract, to ensure that the targets engage in favorable behavior. This study explores the implementation of supply chain integration, by aligning incentives of all the partners involved. This is done through inter-firm sharing of joint profits and beneficial information, aimed at incentive alignment. The following discussion involves an analysis of the sharing of information on market competition and the allocation of joint profit across supply chains.

3.2. Sharing information about new product development performance

Fabless firms (i.e., firms without fabrication facilities) utilize their time and managerial resources, for the development, and, marketing of innovative products while outsourcing manufacturing to EMS providers, who need to successfully achieve innovation of products and production technology. Thus, EMS providers are well positioned to build inter-firm relationships with highly competitive fabless firms. In a fabless supply chain, adopting a very aggressive approach to new product development is crucial to maintaining the inter-firm network's competitive advantage, and, the participants' increased profitability. Successful new product development in fabless supply chains cannot be achieved without strong and reliable commitment between fabless firms and EMS providers.

According to Monteverde (1995), inter-firm technical dialogue in vertical integration benefits technological innovation of new product development and new manufacturing technology. Thus, sharing of knowledge among supply chain partners, comprising parts suppliers, finished product assemblers, and marketers, can create very attractive products.

Only through cooperation among themselves, can fabless firms and EMS providers develop and sell innovative finished products. If fabless supply chains continue supplying attractive new products, they can boost profits of both the fabless firms, and, EMS providers. Thus, an important strategic agenda in the fastest-growing industries is to develop strong competitive advantage through new product development. Therefore, both fabless firms and EMS providers must place a high level of importance on providing highly competitive and innovative products for customers in the market. One of the most significant issues facing fabless firms and EMS providers is the selection of, and alliance with, technologically competitive suppliers or buyers, thereby collectively and collaboratively delivering new finished products into emerging markets.

A beneficial managerial practice for fabless supply chain strategy is to measure a new product's competitiveness. New product competitiveness contributes toward determining, the extent to which the fabless firms, and, EMS providers are successful in achieving their aim of building and participating in fabless supply chains. A strategy-driven performance indicator is the new sales ratio, which is measured as the ratio of current annual sales of new products to total annual sales (Whiteley *et al.*, 1998, p. 20). Whiteley *et al.* (1998) studied the usefulness of the new sales ratio in measuring R&D performance. Fabless supply chain partners are required to determine the target new sales ratio and to control the actual performance across the fabless supply chain in accordance with it.

Assume that a supply chain failed to achieve the goal for new sales ratio in spite of introducing a new high-tech product. The following modification can be made from the perspective of value-based pricing: The parties in the supply chain need to examine whether the sale price of the new high-tech product's sales price is less than customer's willingness to pay. That is, the supply chain must find out if the customer is willing to pay more money than the sales price for buying the new product. This convinces the parties in the supply chain that they must avoid profit-loss resulting from pricing their product lower than customers' willingness-to-pay. Furthermore, parties in the supply chain need to determine whether or not customers understand the value of the new product. Pricing for profit is based on customers' perceived value of the product.

4. Relationship-Specific Investment Strategy in Fabless Supply Chains

4.1. Effects of relationship-specific investments on competitive advantages in fabless supply chains

By outsourcing the manufacturing of new products to EMS providers, fabless firms can channelize capital investments into new product development. Likewise, EMS providers can use capital investments for the fabrication of excellent new finished products. Thus, by allying with each other, fabless firms, and, EMS providers can bring new products to markets.

Therefore, capital investments undertaken by fabless firms and EMS providers become largely specialized, since they are used for a single purpose — either product development or fabrication. Specialized investments in a supply chain are relationship-specific, and the return on these investments depends on cooperation and partnerships among firms in the supply chain dedicated to the growth and competitiveness of the inter-firm network (Crawford, 1990). Capital investments made by each participant in an inter-firm network is conducive to increasing the effectiveness of the business activities of participants, thereby increasing overall profitability of the network. Therefore, relationship-specific investments can be a source of competitive advantage over rivals.

A key factor in supply chain success is reciprocal relationship-specific investments among all participants aimed at activities that generate increased customer value. The strategic value of tangible and intangible investments specialized toward R&D is significantly greater during the growth stage of the product life cycle than it is at any other stage. Innovative new products with a huge demand are in the growth stage of the technology life cycle, in which there is particularly huge potential for product innovation. Highly progressive product innovation on the supply side can further expand the market demand for the release of new products. Hence, growing products can facilitate product technology breakthroughs. At the same time, markets for growing products regularly generate an increased demand for new products, making it impossible for firms to survive unless they continue to release new products. This competitive environment inevitably mandates an increase in R&D investments. Fabless supply chains are characterized by the considerable strategic value of relationship-specific investments made to satisfy fast-changing consumer demand for new products. What is the most effective management practice for fabless supply chains to use in executing reciprocal new product development investment among partners? This study examines the switching cost incurred by fabless firms (EMS providers) when they change their EMS providers (fabless firms).

4.2. Characteristics of relationship-specific investments

Relationship-specific investments in fabless supply chains are devoted to building and supporting activities of fabless firms and EMS providers. Such investments are a source of competitive advantages in fabless supply chains. However, relationship-specific, tangible and intangible assets are of little value when applied to other business relationships. To mitigate risk, fabless supply chains need to make relationship-specific investments based on the real options view of multistage investments over the whole investment life cycle (see Chapter 3). A multistage investment approach is capable of capturing the strategic flexibility to continue or discontinue projects after future cash flow uncertainty has been substantially resolved in accordance with new information that emerged in a publication (Panayi and Trigeorgis, 1998, p. 676).

4.3. Effects of market price

According to the concept of value-based pricing (Hinterhuber, 2004, p. 769), a new product price is the total amount of the following two values: the price of a competitive product that a consumer views as the best alternative and the consumer's perceived value of all attributes that differentiate the product from its competitors.

From the perspective of the value-based pricing approach, the price of manufactured product determined by an EMS provider is affected by two factors, namely, the extent to which new products developed by fabless firms attract consumers and the extent to which the production technology of the EMS provider satisfies consumers. The price of fabless firms is, likewise, influenced by the following factors: production technology of EMS providers, and high-powered R&D of fabless firms. Put differently, the following equation shows the primary factors of finished product prices in fabless supply chains.

Prices of finished product of fabless firms = f (production technology capabilities of the EMS providers, R&D strength of the fabless firms).

In fabless supply chains in which EMS providers offer their manufactured products to fabless firms as finished-product makers, consumer's price-acceptance for the finished products depends on two factors. The first factor is the excellent production technology EMS providers. The second factor is the high-powered R&D of fabless firms. These factors drive the innovative functionality of the finished products; thereby determine the value assigned by customers, and also their willingness pay.

Thus, the market price of a fabless firm's finished product, characterized by high technology, is also an indication of the best technological practice prevalent in high-tech product industries. This means that the market price is an essential parameter in selecting and switching business partners.

5. Allocation of Joint Profit in Fabless Supply Chains

5.1. Effects of joint profit allocation

It is important to allocate joint supply chain profit among supply chain participants as a way of motivating firms with competitive advantages to participate in the supply chain (Monden, 2009). The allocation of a supply chain's joint profit can motivate participants to behave in the interest of the supply chain as a whole, thereby, ultimately increasing their shares of the profit. The level of mutual cooperation among participants of the supply chain depends considerably on how fairly and equally profits of the supply chain are shared among its members. Therefore, the appropriate allocation of a supply chain's joint profits motivates participants to focus on maximizing the supply chain's total profits.

5.2. Market price-based transfer pricing in supply chains that supply growing products

The most important business agenda for supply chains is to achieve a growth rate that is higher than that of total market demand. While the technology embodied in a finished product stays in the growth stage of the technology life cycle, the total market demand for the finished products can grow drastically. The higher the total market demand for a finished product, the bigger is the profit-gap between supply chains that can commercialize their new products swiftly and cheaply, and those that fail to do so. Therefore, whether a fabless supply chain can gain a competitive advantage over other supply chains substantially relies on how well its participants (i.e., fabless firms and EMS providers) can outperform their competitors in terms of commercializing new products. To keep up their competitive advantage in growing markets, fabless firms must keep innovating new products with sophisticated designs, and high customer value, and EMS providers must fabricate the highest-quality products. Moreover, fabless supply chains must achieve the highest possible sales of a finished product by surpassing their competitors in terms of product innovation.

How can the creation of products with high customer value boost profits drastically? This happens when consumers are willing to pay higher prices for innovative products. Measuring the degree of contribution that fabless firms and EMS providers make toward increasing the profitability of the whole fabless supply chain should be based on market price, since market price is affected principally by the result of competition in the market. Fabless supply chains, as mentioned earlier, compete mainly on new product development. Thus, the market price is as a result of competition among fabless supply chains that are driven by new product innovation. Market-based transfer pricing is used for measuring organizational performance of participants in a supply chain. Based on this, individual fabless firms, and EMS providers should make an appropriate decision on whether to continue the ongoing partnership or switch to another partner. They must effectively execute a study on the differences between the profit earned through continuation of transacting with the present partner, and, the potential profit incurred as result of switching partnerships. This can be determined by measuring the profits of fabless firms and EMS providers, using the market prices of finished or manufactured products offered by fabless firms and EMS providers, respectively.

Transfer price for EMSs' manufactured products refers to the value realized when firms sell the products in the external market. Transfer price can be determined using a value-based pricing approach. Assuming that prices in external purchase markets and those in external selling markets are equal, the respective profits of fabless firm and EMS provider-based new product businesses can be calculated as follows:

$$X = a \times b \times (c - d - e) - (f + g), \qquad (5.1)$$

where X is a fabless firm's profit earned from specific new product business, a is the total market demand for a new product, b is the firm's market share for the new product, c is the finished product market price for the new product, d is the variable cost of goods sold per unit, including purchase cost for an EMS provider's manufactured product, e is the unit's variable selling cost, f is the direct capacity cost, and g is the apportioned capacity cost. One strategic goal of the fabless supply chain is to create high-end products that customers are willing to pay a high price for, which increases the value of c in the Equation (5.1).

$$Y = h \times (i - j - k) - (l + m), \qquad (5.2)$$

where Y is the EMS provider's profit earned from specific new product business, h is the quantity of products sold to a fabless firm, i is the product's market prices, j is the variable cost of goods sold per unit, k is the unit's variable selling cost, l is the direct capacity cost, and m is the apportioned capacity cost (Minagawa, 2016).

What is the strategic value of the above-mentioned market-based transfer price for EMS providers' manufactured products in determining profits of supply chain partners? This study considers fabless supply chains in which an EMS provider is responsible for fabricating high-powered goods based on drawings supplied by the fabless firm. The EMS providers need to develop high-quality production technology aimed at enhancing product quality and thus increasing customer value, which in turn increases the fabless firms' reputation in the markets. This enables an increase in orders from the fabless firms. However, when a fabless firm demands that it be able to purchase an EMS provider's product at a price less than the market price for the product, the rational choice for the EMS provider is to engage in transactions with other fabless firms instead. Fabless firms are willing to purchase an EMS provider's products at the market price, provided that the quality of the products is sufficiently attractive. Therefore, when an EMS provider's products fail to satisfy the requirement of fabless firms, the latter should switch transaction partners.[1] The price in the EMS's market is the minimum price that the EMS provider requires to maintain an ongoing relationship with the current fabless partner.

5.3. Fabless supply chains that supply mature products

An increase in the sales of products in the maturity stage of the product life cycle can no longer be expected. Profit during the maturity stage depends largely on complete reduction in profit forgone due to unfulfilled orders and on cost control throughout all business operations.

Therefore, all participants in supply chains that market mature products must collaborate to reduce costs across the supply chains. Increased profitability in supply chains that supply mature products cannot be achieved without effective cost reduction. It is important to allocate among supply chain participants, any additional profit that is gained as a result of inter-participant cooperative cost reduction; this serves to motivate the participants to reduce supply chain costs. What rules should be followed in the allocation of joint profits in supply chains serving mature product markets? The most effective rule regarding the inter-participant

---

[1] Here, the concept of individual rationality in cooperative game theory was applied successfully to switching cost-oriented analysis. I owe that suggestion entirely to Professor Monden (Tsukuba University).

allocation of joint profit is based on cost. Joint profit is allocated among participants based on their activity costs. Increased joint profit earned through cooperative activities by individual participants is allocated among participants according to the costs they incurred through their activities. One practice for cost management in mature product businesses is functional shiftability. In order that supply chains may efficiently achieve customer satisfaction, they must decide which participant is best suited to perform which functions in the supply chain, and then allocate responsibility accordingly. This is the role of functional shiftability (Mallen, 1973). Functional shiftability is more feasible in well-integrated, trust-based supply chains than in arm's length transactions. However, functional shiftability in supply chains typically brings about an increase in the operational costs of participants who have to carry out new tasks that were previously accomplished by other participants. Therefore, the focal firm of a supply chain must create incentives for participants to accept functional shiftability in spite of the increased costs involved. Among these, incentive is the allocation of joint profit to participants across the supply chain. Successful cooperative management across a supply chain, including functional shiftability, requires the allocation of the supply chain's joint profit in proportion to the participants' costs. A supply chain's joint profit can be determined as follows:

$$Z = o - p - q - r - s, \qquad (5.3)$$

where Z is joint profit, o is amount of sales for finished products sold by a fabless firm, p is total variable cost in the fabless firm, except for the cost of purchasing the EMS provider's manufactured products, q is total variable cost of the EMS provider, r is total sum of direct capacity cost and apportioned capacity cost in the fabless firm, and s is total sum of direct capacity cost and apportioned capacity cost in the EMS provider (Minagawa, 2016). A fabless supply chain that supplies mature products must achieve cost reduction across the overall supply chain to increase the joint profit.

The allocation of the joint profit in proportion to participants' costs generates equal shares in terms of the per-unit cost for all participants (Dudek, 2003, p. 134).

6. Conclusion

Cooperative reciprocal investments in product innovation and cost reduction across fabless supply chains drive a higher business performance of fabless firms and EMS providers. This study explored useful ways to facilitate investment by fabless firms and EMS providers. First, the transparency of the new sales ratio across fabless supply chains is beneficial. Second, carrying out market-based transfer price-oriented measurement of participants' performance allows for the best use of their investments.

References

Asanuma, B. (1988). *Manufacturer–Supplier Relationships in Japan and the Concept of Relation-Specific Skill*, Working Paper, No. 2, Kyoto University, Faculty of Economics.

Crawford, V. P. (1990). Relationship-Specific Investment, *The Quarterly Journal of Economics*, Vol. 105, No. 2, pp. 561–574.

Dudek, G. (2003). *Collaborative Planning in Supply Chains*, Heidelberg: Springer-Verlag.

Hinterhuber, A. (2004). Towards Value-Based Pricing — An Integrative Framework for Decision Making, *Industrial Marketing Management*, Vol. 33, No. 8, pp. 765–778.

Holmström, B. (1982). Moral Hazard in Teams, *The Bell Journal of Economics*, Vol. 13, No. 2, pp. 324–340.

Mallen, B. (1973). Functional Spin-Off: A Key to Anticipating Change in Distribution Structure, *Journal of Marketing*, Vol. 37, No. 3, pp. 18–25.

Maloni, M. and Benton, W. C. (2000). Power Influences in the Supply Chain, *Journal of Business Logistics*, Vol. 21, No. 1, pp. 49–73.

Minagawa, Y. (2016). How to Facilitate Inter-Firm Cooperation in a Fabless Global Supply Chain, in *Lean Management of Global Supply Chain*, edited by Monden, Y. and Minagawa, Y., Singapore: World Scientific, pp. 47–65.

Monden, Y. (2009). *Inter-Firm Management Control Systems Based on "Incentive Price": A Profit-Allocation Scheme for Inter-Firm Cooperation*, Tokyo: Zeimu Keiri Kyokai.

Monteverde, K. (1995). Technical Dialog as an Incentive for Vertical Integration in the Semiconductor Industry, *Management Science*, Vol. 41, No. 10, pp. 1624–1638.

Panayi, S. and Trigeorgis, L. (1998). Multi-Stage Real Options: The Cases of Information Technology Infrastructure and International Bank Expansion, *The Quarterly Review of Economics and Finance*, Vol. 38, Special Issue, pp. 675–692.

Perloff, J. M. (2008). *Microeconomics* (5th Edition), Boston: Pearson/Addison-Wesley.

Whiteley, R., Parish, T., Dressler, R., and Nicholson, G. (1998). Evaluating R&D Performance: Using the New Sales Ratio, *Research Technology Management*, Vol. 41, No. 5, pp. 20–22.

Williamson, O. E. (1985). *The Economic Institutions of Capitalism: Firms, Markets, Relational Contracting*, New York: The Free Press.

Chapter 6

Profit Allocation between Assemblers and Parts Suppliers: A Normative Perspective

1. Introduction

A conceptual framework of this study is partly based on Porter's competitive strategy (1985). Porter (1985) shows that the profitability of an industry is a determinant of individual firms. This is true in the case of supply chain member firms' performance. Each partner's profitability is influenced by the performance of the entire supply chain. This implies that the growth of partners requires, above all, enhanced profitability of the entire supply chain.

A key driver for the sustainable growth of supply chains is their joint profit maximization. To achieve this, supply chains must be able to effectively motivate their participants to behave in the best interest of joint profit maximization. Terpend and Krause (2015) propose that incentives fall under two main categories: competitive incentives and cooperative incentives. Competitive incentives refer to instances when suppliers are awarded in business based on how they perform relative to other suppliers. Cooperative incentives refer to sharing an inter-firm network's overall profits generated by the participants' joint performance. The study examines the effects of profit allocation in the supply chains comprising parts suppliers and end product manufacturers.

According to Asanuma's study on the Japanese automobile industry, parts suppliers are classified mainly into two types: "drawing supplied" (DS) parts suppliers and "drawing approved" (DA) parts suppliers. Car makers provide drawings to parts suppliers. These DS parts suppliers then manufacture automobile parts according to the drawings created and supplied by the car makers. These suppliers are responsible for manufacturing those parts (Asanuma, 1988, p. 15). DA parts suppliers manufacture parts according to the drawings that are created by the respective suppliers themselves and then approved by core firms (Asanuma, 1988).

The remainder of the study examines the advantages of distributing joint profits in the two types of supplier-buyer relationships: DS parts suppliers and an end product manufacturer, as well as DA parts suppliers and a finished product manufacturer. The study examines the traits of DS and DA parts from the perspective of the product life cycle. DS parts and DA parts are recognized in this study as being at a mature and at an early stage of the product life cycle, respectively.

2. Two Types of Parts Suppliers

DS parts suppliers need to reduce manufacturing costs while conforming to specifications issued by car makers. In view of this, it is important to establish production processes to reduce manufacturing costs (Asanuma, 1988, pp. 25–26). This perspective of the traits of DS parts is consistent with the argument that these parts are mature elements of the product life cycle. These parts are used as segments of standardized products that must be priced as low as possible and this justifies that DS parts are at a maturity stage. Moreover, designing standardized parts can be accomplished by car makers who are inherently irresponsible in dealing with parts.

The relationships of DA parts suppliers with car makers are deployed in the following way. DA parts suppliers have the potential to design parts that can meet the specifications conveyed by the car maker. After DA parts suppliers have created drawings according to the specifications, they submit them to the car maker. The car maker reviews whether the drawings can be approved. DA parts suppliers are then responsible for manufacturing the parts according to the drawings approved by the car maker (Asanuma, 1988, p. 15).

Therefore, DA parts suppliers must hold the following ability to be rated highly by the car maker. They must develop and manufacture successfully, within a limited-time, high-quality parts according to the specifications issued by the car maker (Asanuma, 1988, p. 27). This strategic characteristic of DA parts is in line with the perspective that DA parts are part of the growth stage of the product life cycle, and the parts suppliers must manufacture high-specification parts as required by the car makers.

3. Improving the Joint Profits of the Entire Supply Chain

This section explains the effects of some managerial control methods to improve supply chain joint profit and then shows the highest-priority drivers of the strategies aimed at increasing this profit.

3.1. Development of highly profitable products

A financial performance indicator that can encourage supply chain participants to behave in the best interest of joint profit is the gross profit net sales ratio of products (gross profit/sales). Improvement in the sales-cost ratio is dependent on cost reduction and value design. The essential concept of value design is shown in the form of the following equation.

$$\text{Value} = \text{Customer-perceived value of the functionality of products or services} / \text{Total cost}$$

The value design aims at raising the customer-perceived value of the functionalities of the products as the value equation numerator. The concept of value design considers that the incremental customer-perceived value of products is greater than the incremental total cost, leading to an increase in net value.

Strategies for achieving high margins include the development of highly differentiated-value products. The product's benefit rests on the assumption that a high pricing strategy is widely accepted in the market, since such a premium-priced product can raise customers' willingness to pay a high price.

A key success factor for developing and supplying high customer-value products efficiently and effectively is to leverage the expertise of the participants including parts suppliers, assemblers, and marketers, and the information on customer needs, to develop highly differentiated, premium value goods.

3.2. Profit improvement through synchronization of goods and information flow

A supply chain, consisting of parts suppliers, finished product manufacturers, distributors, and marketers, suffers fluctuations much more significantly than a separate firm does. Examples include demand fluctuations, supplier delivery quantities, and quality of goods manufactured by supply chain participants (Pullim, 2002; Knowles *et al.*, 2005). Moreover, fluctuations early in the supply chains tend to amplify further down the line (Knowles *et al.*, 2005, p. 54).

Based on Lee *et al.* (1997), one cause of variability that significantly affects supply chain performance is the fluctuation in demand for the finished product. Market changes have negative effects on both supply chain performance and participants' profits. The reasons are as follows. The fluctuation in demand for the finished product can generate variances between orders placed by a retailer to suppliers and the retail store's actual sales of products. It is likely that the retailer's orders will not coincide with the actual retail sales due to the fluctuation (Lee *et al.*, 1997, p. 546). Such a phenomenon is termed as demand distortion (Lee *et al.*, 1997, p. 546). Furthermore, the volume of orders placed by supply chain participants to the next upstream suppliers varies greatly as they move up the supply chain, away from the retailer (Lee *et al.*, 1997, p. 546). This is termed as variance amplification (Lee *et al.*, 1997, p. 546). A phenomenon causing both demand distortion and variance amplification is known as the bullwhip effect (Lee *et al.*, 1997).

An unsuccessful elimination of the bullwhip effect causes excessive cost and loss of sales. The failure to adjust production volume promptly with declining demands engenders excessive stock. Moreover, the failure to reduce time to delivery of finished products to the customer in accordance with the rapid increase in demand results in loss of sales (Knowles *et al.*, 2005, p. 54).

Gaining and sustaining competitive advantage by supply chain participants rely on their lean responses to changes in the demand for finished products. There are two issues to address when dealing with swings in the demand for finished products. The first is how sales loss in times of growing demand can be avoided. The second is how to reduce the risk of excessive inventories as the demand decreases. Regardless of a slow down or unexpected surge in demand, firms must by no means increase sales while reducing inventory-related costs.

The extent of both increase in sales and reduction in inventory-driven costs can be measured effectively through the following financial indicator: inventory carrying cost/sales. Inventory carrying costs usually comprise the opportunity costs of investment tied up in the inventory and the relevant costs of storage, including space rental, spoilage, deterioration, and material handling (Horngren *et al.*, 1994, p. 814). Sales are calculated as follows:

$$\text{Sales} = \text{The total quantity of in coming orders within a period}$$
$$\times \text{Order fill rates} \times \text{Selling prices of the products}$$

A factor for increasing sales is order fill rates. It can be improved by minimizing order fulfillment lead-times measured as the mean time from the date the order is placed to the date the customer receives the shipment (Meyr *et al.*, 2000, p. 35).

There are two issues related to lead time reduction. The first is establishing collaborative production management in the supply chain. Specifically, firms must formulate a finished product manufacturing schedule and a production plan for compliance with such a schedule. A key to solve the problem is to share via the Internet, supply-chain-wide information on orders received by downstream firms responsible for selling finished products and on anticipated orders for these products.

This enables effective component deployment for manufacturing finished products. An order entry information system is an important element of a well-integrated supply chain's collaborative production management solution. A good example of this system is Toyota (Monden, 1994, pp. 75–87).

The second issue in terms of reducing lead-times is the successful implementation of "design for manufacturability" for finished products and components needed to assemble the finished products. Design for manufacturability is an engineering technique to design products in a way such that they are easy to manufacture at low cost (Dean and Susman, 1989).

The minimizing of time to shipment and delivery of finished products requires cooperation among supply chain participants.

3.3. Inter-firm sharing of successful cost-improvement practices

According to Monteverde (1995), inter-firm technical dialog in vertical integration aids technological innovation for new product development and new manufacturing technology. Monteverde's study endorses supply chain cost savings through knowledge sharing among participants.

For implementing the supply-chain-wide transfer of partners' successful practices for cost control, it is important to leverage Activity-Based Costing (ABC) throughout the supply chain (Cokins, 2001). In a cost-improvement approach using ABC across the supply chain, all participants identify and measure activity cost drivers for individual operations and interface operations among them. A cost driver triggers a change in the cost of an activity (Kaplan and Cooper, 1997). Supply chain participants then determine activity cost functions for operations using the cost drivers concerned. Sharing activity cost data across the supply chain helps in easily and effectively identifying cost-improvement measures for each participant through the cost driver analysis of the operation activities. It also helps in effectively and efficiently transferring good practices for cost improvements to other participants through the supply-chain-wide use of ABC functions. Finally, it helps in successfully managing participants' joint costs for the interface operations across the supply chain.

3.4. Functional shiftability-driven supply chain performance improvement

The functional analysis of a supply chain management process aims to investigate all supply chain activities linked to customer demand and then reassign functional responsibilities to the participants who can perform them most effectively (LaLonde and Pohlen, 1996, p. 5). The transfer of responsibility is referred to as "functional shiftability" (Mallen, 1973). Functional shiftability initiates long-term partnerships among firms in a supply chain and does not apply to arm's length relationships between unrelated firms.

Well-integrated supply chains can swiftly and effectively link all activities performed by upstream and downstream partners to meet customer demand. The shortest time to market and the lowest total supply chain costs can be achieved successfully if all supply chain activities are carried out by partners who are best positioned to conduct them. Additionally, a network-wide collaborative review of the degree of integration of supply chain activities performed by each partner and the systemic improvement of supply chain integration can enhance the performance of the entire supply chain. Therefore, transferring responsibilities for specific supply chain functions among partners is a valuable method for improving the performance of the supply chain. This transfer of responsibilities must be done only after ensuring that partners know how to carry out their activities.

One functional shiftability-driven managerial practice is vendor-managed inventory (VMI) that shifts the responsibility of inventory replenishment at retail stores to finished product manufacturers. Put differently, VMI is a collaborative strategy, where upstream firms in the supply chain centralize the management of inventory (Ahrens and Zhou, 2013, p. 24).

Figures 6.1 and 6.2 compare VMI-driven processes with traditional (non-VMI) inventory control processes.

An instrument for determining the optimal resource consumption costs of organizational activities is ABC. It traces and assigns the costs of resource usage to the activities using resource cost drivers (Kaplan and Cooper, 1997). The resource cost drivers link expenditures to activities

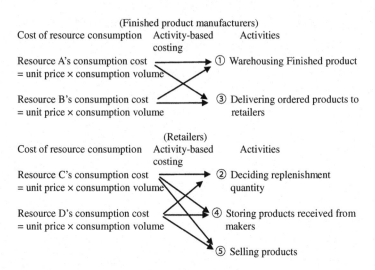

Figure 6.1.   Role sharing in non-VMI inventory replenishment processes

Notes:

1. Based on Kulp (2002), concerning inventory control activities.

2. ①–⑤ Show supply-chain-wide inventory control steps.

3. Makers consume resources A and B; retailers use resources C and D.

4. Arrows show tracing and assigning of resource expenses to activities performed.

performed. The allocation of resource consumption is based on the resource cost-driver rate as calculated by dividing the total cost of the resources by the total number of resource cost drivers.

Figure 6.1 shows the non-VMI approach for inventory replenishment, under which retailers have no responsibility for sharing private information about the demand for their finished products with makers (Kulp, 2002). Meanwhile, retailers who commit themselves to VMI, provide their private demand-related information to finished product manufacturers, thereby, leaving the manufacturers in charge of replenishment at the retail stores. Makers engage themselves in replenishing the retailers' stock of finished products using the demand information received from the retailers. Therefore, VMI can relieve retailers from sending their orders to the makers. A comparison of costs incurred before and after VMI introduction, as shown in Figures 6.1 and 6.2, is required to

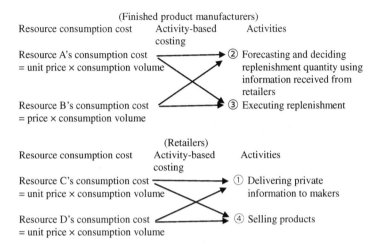

Figure 6.2.   Role sharing in VMI-initiated inventory replenishment processes

Notes:

1. Based on Kulp (2002), concerning VNI-initiated inventory control activities.

2. ①–④ Show supply-chain-wide inventory control steps.

3. Makers consume resources A and B; retailers use resources C and D.

4. Arrows show tracing and assigning resource expenses to activities performed.

ensure that a right decision, concerning whether VMI should be introduced, is taken.

Ahrens and Zhou (2013) represent the use of VMI as a global competitive advantage of Lenovo, a Chinese PC maker. Under VMI, raw material suppliers must swiftly replenish production in the Lenovo manufacturing plants (Ahrens and Zhou, 2013, p. 24).

Functional shiftability and the resultant operational improvement throughout the entire supply chain is key to reducing overall supply chain costs. However, functional shiftability in a supply chain is not easy to carry out. A critical success factor for functional shiftability is establishing a network-wide win-win relationship, thereby enabling all the partners of the chain to benefit from it. Transferring functional responsibility can decrease the supply chain's total costs. Nevertheless, partners who were given additional tasks due to functional shiftability may see a rise in their own costs. Partners resist from performing additional tasks assigned to them using functional shiftability that provide no return. To overcome the "disincentive" problem, it is beneficial to introduce the allocation of the supply chain's joint profit among partners. The next section completes the discussion on the effects of joint profit sharing across the supply chain.

As shown above, a network-wide leveraging of other partners' expertise and knowledge, largely and positively affects the profits of the entire network. Therefore, the study examines the most appropriate rules to allocate the joint profit of the supply chain among the participants, so as to promote collaborative knowledge sharing across the supply chain and increase the joint profits.

4. Life-Cycle-Based Competitiveness Analysis

Porter (1985) set out the generic strategies that are subdivided into "differentiation," "cost leadership," and "focus" (offering a specialized service in a niche market). The following discussion is on the impacts of product life cycle on differentiation-focused and cost-leadership-focused strategies.

An essential requirement in the success of differentiation strategies is that technology embedded in the goods is at the fluid stage of its life cycle. During this stage, technology innovation tends to happen rapidly and frequently. A differentiation strategy aims mainly at creating uniquely valuable products or services to increase consumers' willingness-to-pay. The main purpose of cost-leadership-focused strategies is to supply a product or service at an affordable price by achieving cost reduction throughout all the business operations. The following discussion considers the impacts of goods' life cycles on differentiation and cost-leadership strategies.

The success requirement in a differentiation strategy is that technology embedded in the products or services is at the fluid stage of its life cycle. In this stage, technological innovation tends to happen rapidly as well as frequently.

An essential success factor in supplying mature goods is adapting to a reduction in market demand. Therefore, the greatest competitive advantage is high-quality operations at lower costs.

5. Effect of Profit Sharing in Supply Chains

Equitable profit allocation methods in supply chains require each partner to be made aware that the received share is worth the efforts taken (Nigro and Abbate, 2011, p. 239). The below discussion considers DS parts supplier-driven and DA parts supplier-driven contributions toward boosting the joint profit of the supply chain. DS parts suppliers should facilitate cost improvement. DA parts suppliers are required to promote launches of new finished products. Hence, the study inquires two different sets of rules of allocating supply chain joint profit: rules helpful in furthering the network-wide cost reduction and rules to promote new product introduction across the supply chain.

6. Allocating Joint Profit among DS Parts Suppliers and Finished Product Manufacturers

6.1. Competitiveness of DS parts-based production in inter-firm networks

Players in charge of designing DS parts are not parts-makers but finished product makers. Therefore, DS parts are designed by finished product manufacturers who are not responsible for manufacturing individual parts. From the DS parts point of view, there is a tendency to believe that these parts are not powered. Rather, DS parts show characteristics of being technologically standardized. Accordingly, one of the missions of DS part suppliers, toward maximizing profits from selling the supply chain's finished products is to cost-effectively and quickly produce high-quality parts (Asanuma, 1988).

It is extremely difficult for finished product manufactures to design components for new products. Instead, parts that finished product manufacturers are able to design are limited to standardized ones. As far as technologically standardized parts are concerned, those who can design the parts pass them to finished product manufacturers with accumulated knowledge about the parts. Finished products assembled with standardized parts are theoretically at the maturity stage in the product technology life cycle. As a result, the competitive advantage of finished products made from standardized parts does not arise from creating new functionality but from establishing cost-leadership and ensuring quick delivery to the customer.

6.2. Profit sharing in a DS parts-based products supply chain

6.2.1. *Impacts of Continued Partnerships on Economics of Scale*

An approach to establish an overall low-cost position in a firm is to attain economies of scale (Hill, 1988). Empirical evidence reveals the cost advantages of production at a minimum efficient scale (MES) (Silberston, 1972; Hill, 1988). MES provides the efficient plant size represented by factors, such as total output over time (Silberston, 1972; Hill, 1988). According to previous research on relationships between the cumulative output of the same product and the unit cost, producing quantities lower than the MES is cost-disadvantageous (Silberston, 1972; Hill, 1988).

Figure 6.3 is a conceptual diagram for increased production-driven cost-reduction in manufacturing the same product. A factor that generates economies of scale, as shown in Figure 6.3, is the effect of high-volume

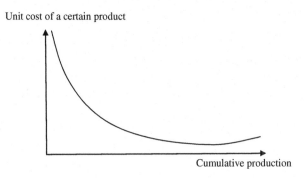

Figure 6.3.   A conceptual diagram for greater cumulative output-driven cost-advantage in the production of the same product

production for the same product. High-volume production enables a firm to ensure continuous output of a certain product. This, in turn, promotes the accumulation of knowledge for the most efficient production practices. Hence, it can be said that cost-improvement practices can be developed through accumulated knowledge.

Therefore, high-volume production allows firms to facilitate cost reductions. A reduction in the production cost of parts by suppliers can be promoted through a long-standing partnership with a certain finished product manufacturer. Parts suppliers can accumulate manufacturing experience and thus achieve cost reduction through a long-term relationship with the same assembler.

6.2.2. *Allocation Rules*

Because DS parts have a trait of being technologically standardized to increase profits, the promotion of cost reduction is a top-priority issue for supply chains that offer finished products produced with DS parts. This subsection will consider the most effective way to allocate supply chain joint profits among DS parts suppliers and finished product manufacturers. This study does not empirically inquire into but rather theoretically and rationally examines the rules of supply chain joint-profit allocation. The main principle of supply chains' joint profit sharing explained in this study lies in allocating the pie extended by the network-wide cost reduction among the partners.

The method of allocating the joint profit of DS parts-based production in inter-firm networks is as follows:

The first step is to carry out supply-chain-wide collaborative ABC and activity analyses across supply chains based on partnerships between the partners. Then, the participants should determine the partners that are best positioned to perform each of the supply chain functions, using information related to functional shiftability generated from the inter-partner ABC exercise.

An important point in the first step is to implement inter-firm ABC before the business year begins, based on activity analyses across a supply chain, with a view to expand its potential for continuous cost reduction at each level of the supply chain. Network-wide ABC driven by activity analyses enables partners to make distinctions between value-added and non-value-added activities across a network and gain a clear understanding of the cost incurred by the chain's members. Network-wide ABC, coupled with activity analyses, allows the partners to conduct a collaborative investigation of functional shiftability across the supply chain.

In addition, the application of supply-chain-wide ABC generally makes activity costs incurred throughout the supply chain open to all partners. This aids in achieving cost transparency in supply chains through information sharing (i.e., the sharing of total supply chain costs). Cost transparency in supply chains can create an inter-partner understanding on how activities performed by each partner affect the total costs and joint profit of the entire supply chain. This can lead to the optimization of all operations across the supply chain. The allocation of the overall joint profit in the supply chain can convince the members to disclose their costs to increase the joint profit.

The second step occurs after a firm has determined the best performer for each activity carried out in the supply chain. In this step, supply chains must determine the standard costs required for the highest level of performance in network-wide activities. It is mandatory that all the partners determine the standard activity costs collaboratively, as this can reduce the risk of opportunistic standard cost setting by self-interested partners.

The third step is the execution of cost reduction by supply chain partners during the business year. All participants of a supply chain must achieve cost reduction.

The fourth step is the calculation of a supply chain's joint profits at the end of the business year. The joint profit of the entire supply chain is calculated by subtracting the total costs incurred by the activities of the partners from the revenue earned from selling finished goods.

The fifth step is the allocation of the joint profit among the supply chain participants. It is important to allocate the joint profit of a supply chain among the participants according to how much they spent on performing the operational activities. This profit sharing method in a supply chain is based on the argument that the monetary amounts of resource consumption incurred by partners' business activities contribute to the network's profit.

Parts suppliers' high-volume production facilitates their knowledge accumulation on supply chain cost reduction. By using the knowledge, parts suppliers can reduce their parts costs. This means that when an assembler continually places high-volume orders with the same parts supplier, it receives the ordered parts at a low cost. Continual transactions between parts suppliers and assemblers initiated by equitable relationships entail well-integrated activities of partners. Under the cost-based joint profit allocation scheme that uses each partner's activity (and activity-based cost) as the basis for allocation, the overall incentive alignment across the supply chain can be achieved easily, as well as remarkably. Activities of supply chain participants contribute to an increase in the supply chain's sustainable growth. An allocation scheme, wherein a network's joint profit is distributed according to the participants' activity costs, considers the contribution of participants' activities to the overall profitability.

Operational inefficiencies in firms trigger extra costs when they use actual costs (instead of standard costs) as a base for allocating profit: the higher the actual costs incurred by the firms, the higher the share of the joint profits. The allocation of supply chain joint profit based on partners' actual costs often motivates them to improve the joint profit of the entire supply chain. It however leads to increased operational inefficiencies throughout the supply chain. This issue can be overcome by applying a standard cost-based profit allocation.

6.3. Market-price-based transfer pricing-driven allocation of joint profit between suppliers of DA parts and finished product manufacturers

DA parts suppliers are fully responsible for warranting quality. By fulfilling the quality warranty responsibility, they obtain discretionary powers to design parts that they produce (Fujimoto, 1997, p. 194). Car makers leave the design of DA parts in the hands of parts suppliers as experts, since DA parts are technologically advanced products.

When new product development requires parts not produced in-house, the manufacturers outsource the parts. In procurement outsourcing, the finished product manufacturers must establish healthy relationships with the parts manufacturing suppliers. The following discussion is regarding the appropriate buyer-supplier selection by finished product manufacturers and DA parts suppliers.

What is the requirement for the most valuable parts suppliers from the context of finished product manufacturers? Finished product manufacturers look for parts suppliers who can design and produce parts that can increase the finished products' customer value. Therefore, the selection of highly capable DA parts suppliers is a dominant agenda in finished product manufacturers' procurement strategy.

Finished product manufacturers must consider including the DA parts-driven innovative value into the buying price of the parts, thereby deepening their relationships with DA parts suppliers and establishing interlocked partnerships. A typical parts pricing practice is to set the price of DA parts as the amount arrived at after adding the reference prices to the premium customer value according to value-based pricing practices. This price for DA parts is presumed to be accepted by customers in the market.

DA parts suppliers must select a finished product manufacturer who is willing to pay a high price for high-value parts produced by them. The DA parts' price, to be realized on exchange in the market, is the floor price acceptable to the DA parts suppliers. This leads to the use of market-price-based transfer pricing between DA parts suppliers and assemblers. If a parts supplier offers parts to an assembler at a lower price than the market price, the suppliers are motivated to discontinue the partnership with the assembler. Observing the transaction from the side of the assembler, a market price for the parts is actually the selling price.

7. Concluding Remarks

The study explored the most effective joint profit allocation methods of a supply chain comprising component suppliers and finished product manufacturers. The research was conducted from the perspective of how to establish a competitive advantage of the entire supply chain based on the product life cycle.

Let us consider that both finished products and components have prominent attributes of a mature market demand. The market condition requires firms to achieve cost advantage as their core competitiveness. A source of cost reduction in product manufacturing is economies of scale. Therefore, high-volume production of a component is more conducive to reduce the component cost. Focusing on finished product makers' competitiveness, continued relationship with the same component supplier is essential to achieve economies of scale. The study examined the effects of cost-based allocation of joint profit on the competitive advantage of supply chain initiated by DS parts.

Let us consider a supply chain initiated by DA parts. What generates the core competitive advantage for firms that find themselves confronted with the race to introduce new products? The market environment encourages firms to have close ties with highly innovative partners. This can render new product development power to component suppliers. The effective selection of the best partners in innovative markets is powered by the application of market-price-based transfer pricing to the intra-supply chain transaction of parts.

References

Ahrens, N. and Zhou, Y. (2013). *China's Competitiveness: Myth, Reality, and Lessons for the United States and Japan: Case Study: Lenovo*, Washington, DC: Center for Strategic and International Studies.

Asanuma, B. (1988). *Manufacturer-Supplier Relationships in Japan and the Concept of Relation-Specific Skill*, Working Paper/Faculty of Economics, No. 2, Kyoto University.

Cokins, G. (2001). Measuring Costs Across the Supply Chain, *Cost Engineering*, Vol. 43, No. 10, pp. 25–31.

Dean, J. W. and Susman, G. I. (1989). Organizing for Manufacturable Design, *Harvard Business Review*, Vol. 67, No. 1, pp. 28–36.

Fujimoto, T. (1997). *The Evolution of a Manufacturing System at Toyota*, Tokyo: Yuhikaku (in Japanese).

Hill, C. W. (1988). Differentiation Versus Low Cost or Differentiation and Low Cost: A Contingency Framework, *Academy of Management Review*, Vol. 13, No. 3, pp. 401–412.

Horngren, C. T., Foster, G., and Datar, S. (1994). *Cost Accounting: A Managerial Emphasis*, New Jersey: Prentice Hall.

Kaplan, R. S. and Cooper, R. (1997). *Cost and Effect: Using Integrated Cost Systems to Drive Profitability and Performance*, Boston: Harvard Business School Press.

Knowles, G., Whicker, L., Femat, H. J., and Del Campo, C. F. (2005). A Conceptual Model for the Application of Six Sigma Methodologies to Supply Chain Improvement, *International Journal of Logistics: Research and Applications*, Vol. 8, No. 1, pp. 51–65.

Kulp, S. C. (2002). The Effect of Information Precision and Information Reliability on Manufacturer-Retailer Relationships, *The Accounting Review*, Vol. 77, No. 3, pp. 653–677.

LaLonde, B. J. and Pohlen, T. L. (1996). Issues in Supply Chain Costing, *The International Journal of Logistics Management*, Vol. 7, No. 1, pp. 1–12.

Lee, H. L., Padmanabhan, V., and Whang, S. (1997). Information Distortion in a Supply Chain: The Bullwhip Effect, *Management Science*, Vol. 43, No. 4, pp. 546–558.

Mallen, B. (1973). Functional Spin-Off: A Key to Anticipating Change in Distribution Structure, *Journal of Marketing*, Vol. 37, No. 3, pp. 18–25.

Meyr, H., Rohde, J., Stadtler, H., and Kilger, C. (2000). Supply Chain Analysis, in *Supply Chain Management and Advanced Planning*, edited by Stadtler, H. and Kilger, C., Berlin: Springer, pp. 29–56.

Monden, Y. (1994). *Toyota Production System: An Integrated Approach to Just-In-Time* (2nd Edition), London: Chapman & Hall.

Monteverde, K. (1995). Technical Dialog as an Incentive for Vertical Integration in the Semiconductor Industry, *Management Science*, Vol. 41, No. 10, pp. 1624–1638.

Nigro, G. L. and Abbate, L. (2011). Risk Assessment and Profit Sharing in Business Networks, *International Journal of Production Economics*, Vol. 131, No. 1, pp. 234–241.

Porter, M. E. (1985). *Competitive Advantage: Creating and Sustaining Superior Performance*, New York: Free Press.

Pullim, J. (2002). Success Comes in Threes, *Professional Engineering*, Vol. 15, No. 8, p. 28.

Silberston, A. (1972). Economics of Scale in Theory and Practices, *Economic Journal*, Vol. 82, No. 325, pp. 369–391.

Terpend, R. and Krause, D. R. (2015). Competition or Cooperation? Promoting Supplier Performance with Incentives under Varying Conditions of Dependence, *Journal of Supply Chain Management*, Vol. 51, No. 4, pp. 29–54.

Chapter 7

Management of Supply Chains Fulfilling the Demand of Mature Goods

1. Introduction

Every product or service has a limited life. All products or services enter the market after going through the growth stage, then the maturity stage, and finally the decline (Abernathy and Utterback, 1978, pp. 40–41). The life cycle of the technology embedded in the goods decides the transition of the product's or service's life cycle. In other words, products or services become saturated as the technology matures. Products or services in the maturity stage are simultaneously in the maturity stage of their embodied technology life cycles. Therefore, mature products or services have little potential for product or service innovation.

This study examines the biggest challenge facing supply chains whose main product or service is in the maturity stage in their life cycles. To elaborate, the supply chains need to capture profit from the sale of their main product or service in the mature markets over a long period, while devoting itself to creating a new product or service. Cash flow from firms' primal goods is a dominant funding source for new products or services development (Hedley, 1977). In other words, how much money supply chains can invest in the development of new products or services largely relies on profit margin from their current main products or services. The more money supply chains earn from selling their existing dominant goods, the more money can be invested in new goods creation.

The principal purpose of the study is to explore how to improve the profitability performance of supply chains selling mature products or services. A key to ensuring the high profitability of final product or service in the mature market is to increase its share of the total demand (a limited pie) at a low cost. From the strategy perspective, a supply chain supplying a mature product or service must avoid missing its opportunity to sell the product or service in markets.

Moreover, the study explores what customer value is to be targeted in supply chains serving mature goods and then examines the effect of throughput accounting practice on the management of mature goods supply chains.

2. Competitive Advantages Through Supply Chains

Supply chain partnership is a dynamic business relationship among diverse participants based on mutual trust, information sharing, shared risk, and rewards (Lambert *et al.*, 1996, pp. 10–11). Considering the management control tools for building a robust partnership, supply chain managers must develop management control systems to integrate a joint strategy into collaborative business plans (Lambert *et al.*, 1996). Collaborative business planning leads to the synchronization of all value chains along the supply chains in order to effectively and efficiently satisfy end-customers' needs.

Joint business planning across a supply chain helps facilitate goal congruence among partners. Effective, faster response to market demand changes is supported by information sharing among those partners. Moreover, a supply chain manager needs to distribute the supply chain's joint profit among participants, thereby motivating them to act in the interest of the supply chain's profit. The allocation of a supply chain's joint profit to the participants can be a powerful management practice that aligns partners' incentives to make business decisions in the interest of total profit increases of the overall supply chain. This helps convince the partners that enhanced joint profit benefits their own profit growth. Goal congruence and incentive alignment in a supply chain complement each other (Bouillon *et al.*, 2006).

Based on deploying a collaborative plan-do-check-action system (management control systems) across the supply chains, participants can synchronize a value chain in each participant in order to achieve a quick response to market demand. Therefore, the adaptability of changing demand is the primary capability of supply chains.

3. Satisfying Customer Needs in Mature Supply Chains

A problem to be solved in the formulation of product strategies is how to create a means to satisfy a certain customer preference. From this perspective, we elaborate on which customer preferences to target in mature supply chains' market-oriented strategies. Focusing on the supply side, customers witness a transition from an early, fluid state to being mature, rigid in the goods life cycle (Abernathy and Utterback, 1978, pp. 41–42; Clark, 1985, pp. 235–236). Based on the life-cycle pattern, markets that are more fluid face a situation where successive firms offer new functionality through new products or services. However, ease of creating new functionality in products or services decreases as goods move from fluid to mature phase in their life cycles.

As in previous researches on customer preferences (Woodside *et al.*, 2008, pp. 8–19; Macdivitt and Wilkinson, 2012, pp. 9–83), they include service benefits (e.g., quick delivery of the right good), the ability of goods to make the buyer or user feel good, and company or brand benefits other than functionality. To effectively and efficiently increase customer value, it is important for mature supply chains to devote their efforts to the creation of better service benefits, and to enhance the ability of products or services to make the buyer or user feel good (see Figure 7.1). It is technologically difficult to create new functionality in a product or service in the mature stage. This study focuses on the on-time delivery of goods needed by customers as a strategic theme in mature supply chains. Supply chains

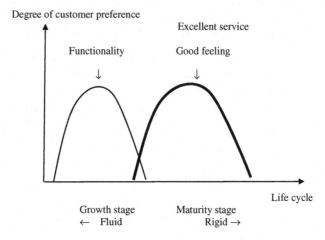

Figure 7.1.   Relationships between customer preference changes and life-cycle movement

Note: Customer preference is based on Woodside *et al.* (2008, p. 9).

in mature markets, in the face of decreased demands due to stagnant innovation, must increase their net cash flow through the quick delivery of products or services to customers.

4. Management of Supply Chains Fulfilling the Demand of Mature Goods

4.1. Critical success factors

4.1.1. *Impacts of Prolonging the Life Cycle of Mature Goods on Funding for Dematurity Projects*

Hedley (1977) created a business or product portfolio model named growth-share matrix based on the product life-cycle theory. It categorizes product portfolio using two dimensions: growth rate of the market and relative market share. The two evaluation indicators are implemented as follows. The higher market share of a firm results in higher cash returns. While high market growth rate means higher earning, firms in such markets are required to invest more capital to achieve further growth. Based on the growth-share matrix, a product can be in one of the four following categories: Stars: high market-share and high market growth; Cash

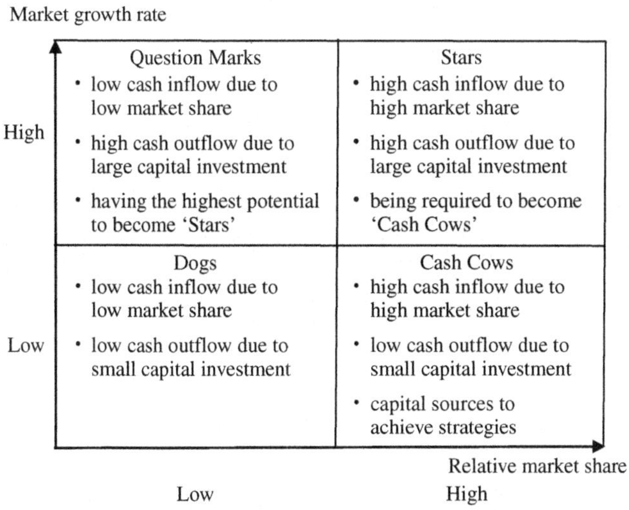

Market growth rate

	Question Marks • low cash inflow due to low market share • high cash outflow due to large capital investment • having the highest potential to become 'Stars'	Stars • high cash inflow due to high market share • high cash outflow due to large capital investment • being required to become 'Cash Cows'
High		
Low	Dogs • low cash inflow due to low market share • low cash outflow due to small capital investment	Cash Cows • high cash inflow due to high market share • low cash outflow due to small capital investment • capital sources to achieve strategies

Relative market share

Low   High

Figure 7.2. The growth-share matrix
Source: Based on Hedley (1977, pp. 10–11).

Cows: high market-share and low market growth; Dogs: low market-share and low market growth; and Question Marks: low market share, high market growth (see Figure 7.2; Hedley, 1977, pp. 10–11).

The growth-share matrix values the relative competitive position of a business or product's cash generation rate (Hedley, 1977, p. 10). Star products need more investment to achieve further growth. Cash cow products are at the maturity stage of the product life cycle; hence, they can hardly encounter an opportunity for capital investment in new goods development projects. As such, competitive cash cow products, namely, cash cow products with high market share, are in a position to generate large cash surplus. This means that the cash cows provide the cash for investment in other section of the company's portfolio. Firms must move stars into cash cows by maintaining the highest competitiveness of their stars product (Hedley, 1977, p. 11).

Competitive mature products in the product life cycle are categorized into cash cows. Due to low product development opportunity, a product or service in the maturity stage requires very little capital investment in radical innovation projects. Hence, high market-share mature product or service can generate cash surplus.

Supply chains whose main products or services are mature in the markets must achieve dematurity by developing new products or services. However, these supply chains require sufficient funds for the creation of new products or services. What is the best source of funding for mature supply chains? Borrowing imposes higher financial risks on firms in mature markets relative to firms in growing markets in terms of financial conditions. Hence, mature supply chains should rely substantially on profit from selling the supply chains' existing mature goods with competitive advantages. Retained earnings are a financial risk-free fund. Thus, the mature supply chains must extend the life cycle of their main products or services, and thereby, increase capital money available for investment to create new products or services (see Figure 7.3). For prolonging the mature period of the life cycle, it is essential to solve the issue of increasing customer satisfaction with mature goods. This problem is examined in the next section.

4.1.2. *Market-Oriented Strategies of Mature Goods*

Products or services in the maturity stage are technologically standardized and, therefore, undifferentiated. If supply chains in mature markets charge their customers a high price, they may lose customer loyalty.

Regarding the key factors of survival in the competition among supply chains fulfilling the demand of mature products or services, this study explores how to enhance the ability to distribute the right goods at the right time to customers. To meet such customer satisfaction requires a

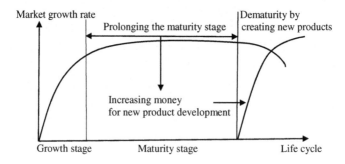

Figure 7.3.   Conceptualizing the effect of prolonging the maturity stage

reduction in lead time, which is defined as time elapsed from the date the order is placed to the date the customer receives the goods ordered. The remainder of the study proves the relevance of throughput accounting to the measurement of performance in mature goods supply chains.

5. Managerial Advantages of Throughput Accounting

Among the influential advocators for throughput accounting are Galloway and Waldron (1988a, 1988b, 1989a, 1989b), who propose that the growth of profits is affected by shortening lead time (Galloway and Waldron, 1988a, pp. 34–35). The curtailment of lead time, in turn, depends directly on inventory level. Low inventory reduces lead time because an increasing inventory queue length at a certain workstation increases the average queuing time, thereby resulting in longer lead time. Therefore, low inventory reduces lead time. As Kilger (2000, p. 212) demonstrated, the effect of lead times' contraction resides in the generation of additional sales. As a result, profitability grows with a decreasing inventory. An increase in inventory often causes a breakdown in many managerial functions. This leads Galloway and Waldron to consider as incorrect, any decision-making that induces increased inventories (Galloway and Waldron, 1989a, p. 33).

The distinctive characteristic of throughput accounting lies in its cost calculation system, under which the intrinsic value of inventories is realized only when sales of inventories are achieved. According to throughput accounting, inventory is best valued at the material cost incurred in producing the inventory until it is sold (Dugdale and Jones, 1998, p. 211). This notion of throughput accounting contrasts markedly with that of conventional absorption costing. Traditional absorption cost systems calculate inventory cost according to cost attachment theory. In calculating the cost of goods in process and cost of finished goods, absorption costing sums up direct labor cost and apportioned overhead expense with material cost in proportion with the stage of manufacturing. To elaborate, in absorption costing, product costs increase with the degree of completion of the manufacturing process.

Throughput accounting does not absorb any cost elements other than direct material cost to manufacturing units. In other words, throughput accounting calculates inventory cost using only direct material cost and, hence, defines all costs incurred in production, other than direct material cost, as period cost.

Figure 7.4 shows that throughput accounting profit is a function of cost of goods sold calculated solely at direct material cost (i.e., variable material cost), throughput contribution, and operating cost. Here, inventorial cost contains only direct material cost. As a result, the cost of goods sold is valued solely at direct material cost. Other costs, namely all the manufacturing costs incurred other than direct material costs plus selling and administrative expenses, are defined as operating cost, which is the period cost. Such costs are always expensed in the same period in which they are incurred. The total period cost incurred within a fiscal year is matched with revenue realized in that same year. As shown in Figure 7.4, revenue minus the cost of goods sold at direct material cost is the throughput contribution.

Table 7.1 shows the comparison between throughput accounting, variable (direct) costing, and absorption costing in terms of how many cost items are summed up to form a product cost. This affects the reported period costs provided that the same costing data are used.

Product cost is calculated and attached to finished product values in both previous and current years. It is used to calculate the value of the

Revenue	XXXX
(−) Cost of goods sold only as direct material cost	XXXX
Throughput Contribution	XXXX
(−) Operating expenses:	
all manufacturing cost except for direct material costs	XXXX
selling and administrative expenses	XXXX
Profit	XXXX

Figure 7.4.   Throughput accounting

Table 7.1.   Comparison of the extent of cost items and period cost

The total amount of cost items summed as a product	Throughput accounting < Variable costing < Absorption costing
Amount of period costs	Throughput accounting > Variable costing > Absorption costing

inventory of finished products until the time of sales. At the time when a product is sold, the value of the units sold is the cost of goods sold. Consequently, given that the quantity of products available for sales within the current year is constant as the amount of unsold inventory grows, the cost of goods sold conversely decreases, which affects the profit growth reported in the income statement.

Excessive production tends to end in an excess of unsold inventory. Nevertheless, overproduction decreases cost of goods sold, leading to a growth of profits reported in the income statement. The high profit reported, due to extra production, is undoubtedly misleading managerially.

However, the notion of how many cost items are combined to derive product cost is associated with the extent to which increased inventory influences the profit recorded in the income statement. The more a product's value decreases, the lesser it impacts the recorded profit. The fewer number of cost items a product cost contains, the smaller the product costs become.

Therefore, costing systems that add more cost items into the product cost prompt managers to increase inventories in order to boost the reported profits in the income statement. In other words, a costing system whose product costs contain fewer cost items discourages managers from building up excessive inventory.

Throughput accounting calculates product cost only with direct material cost. Hence, throughput accounting yields the lower inventoriable costs than variable and absorption costing, given that these costing approaches use common data. In other words, an average unit product cost under throughput accounting is typically lower than that under variable and absorption costing. Accordingly, throughput accounting is of considerable importance managerially in that it can mitigate the incentive to overproduce. When a firm performs excess production over actual demand, in relation to other costing approaches, throughput accounting provides the smaller excessive amount of inventory cost caused by overproduction. This means that throughput accounting is helpful to reduce the motivation of firms to perform excessive production over actual demand in order to reduce the cost of sold goods relatively, thereby increasing profit.

Considering the comparison of the amount of period cost in Table 7.1, throughput accounting is the largest. This poses a problem; boosting profit requires a sufficient increase in sales to recover period cost. However, when a firm fails to capture a volatile demand in mature markets, throughput accounting leads it to an unsuccessful recovery of period cost, and a resultant deficit loss.

5.1. How to improve throughput contribution

There are two means to increase throughput contribution. The first approach is concerned with high pricing strategies. A customer is willing to pay higher price for buying more innovative goods. A price increase has the potential toward boosting profit. The attainability of high pricing to increase profit relies on whether a product or service is able to offer innovative functionality that can attract more customers. To elaborate, the successful high pricing of products or services requires appropriate high functionality for their high price. Therefore, the high pricing strategy is never right for mature goods.

The second approach to increase throughput contribution aims to achieve quick delivery of the right goods to customers at low cost. This is an appropriate means for mature goods. The net income of throughput accounting is determined largely by the throughput contribution. Shortening the lead time adds to throughput contribution. On-time delivery, in turn, helps additional sales yield (Kilger, 2000, p. 212). Firms that cannot respond to market changes quickly face a decrease in throughput contribution, thereby jeopardizing the recovery of their operating expenses. Thus, throughput accounting signals the achievement of a quick response to demand changes.

6. Transfer Pricing Based on Throughput Accounting

For supply chains offering mature products or services to consumers, timely delivery is the key to the survival. Accordingly, throughput accounting is relevant to successful management of mature goods supply chains. Transfer pricing for transactions between the supply chain partners is included among supply chain management practices. Transactions between partners are different from pure arm's length transactions, and, therefore, may have a separate transfer pricing policy.

With regard to the transfer pricing for supply chains, this study uses a throughput accounting ratio, namely, throughput contribution/operating costs. The operating cost of throughput accounting contributes toward earning throughput contribution. A factor of increasing throughput contribution is higher finished goods turnover. Therefore, the throughput contribution per operating costs (i.e., throughput contribution/operating costs) increases by boosting the turnover of finished goods while reducing the operation cost. A key to improve turnover is quick responses to market changes. Thus, the following transfer pricing is useful.

$$T = \frac{x}{y} \times a + b,$$

where T is transfer price, which will be applied to a selling partner's sales for the entirety of the following year to a buying partner, x is this year's annual throughput contribution that the selling partner has earned through its sales to the buying partner, y is this year's annual amount of the selling partner's operating costs that has been driven by its sales to the buying partner, a is the selling partner's standard unit average operating costs for the following year's planned annual volume of transactions with the buying partner, b is the selling partner's standard unit direct material cost for the following year's planned annual volume of transactions with the buying partner.

For this transfer pricing model, the selling partner's standard unit average operating costs, as well as the unit direct material costs for the following year's planned annual amount of transactions with the buying partner, needs to be determined. These two standard costs are part of the proposed transfer price, and, hence, affect the partners' profits for the following year. With regard to how the two standard costs are predetermined, negotiations between the related partners are regarded as the norm. However, this means that the transfer prices cannot be determined soon after supply chains begin. Rather, a market price is used as the transfer price during the first year after supply chains are established.

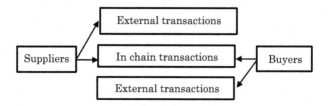

Figure 7.5.   In chain and external transactions in supply chain participants

Performance measurement in supply chains, here, requires the respective supply chain partners to separate the operating costs incurred within the inter-partner transactions from those resulting from external transactions (including arm's length transactions). For supply chain partners to identify operating costs that are driven by inter-partner transactions, it is important for them to use activity-based costing (Demmy and Talbott, 1998). Activity-based costing assigns resource consumption amount incurred in firms to activities ranging from the procurement of materials, to the delivery of goods to customers through different transactions (Figure 7.5).

The rest of this section shows how the transfer pricing outlined above can help efficiently manage supply chains. The analysis sheds light on the impact of both throughput contribution and operating costs for the partners on the transfer prices, holding other variables constant. Under the proposed transfer pricing model, the more the selling partners raise the excess of their throughput contribution over their incurred operating costs, the higher the following year's transfer prices become. For the selling partners, maintaining the higher transfer price has a positive impact on the growth of their revenues.

Further, an increase in a partner's throughput contribution depends mainly on the curtailment of lead times in supply chains. Hence, the value of proposed transfer pricing lies in increasing the motivation of all partners to boost supply chain profit by improving lead time.

The proposed transfer pricing model prompts the entire supply chain to cooperate in reducing the lead times. This is because transfer pricing hinges largely on the throughput contribution of the selling partners. Among the most important drivers of the enhanced throughput contribution of the selling partners is shortened lead time. Here, what should not be overlooked is the fact that the negative effect of prolonged lead times in a certain part of a supply chain is likely to easily spread throughout the whole partnership. Thus, partners' profits depend on whether or not each of the partners can reduce their lead times into a managerially acceptable level. This, in turn, creates incentives for all partners to cooperate in preventing deteriorations in lead time from taking place under any of the supply chain partners.

7. Concluding Remarks

The study showed the effects of throughput accounting as a performance measurement tool in mature supply chains. Furthermore, the study explored the motivational effects of transfer pricing based on throughput accounting information to integrate supply chain participants into successfully solving managerial issues faced by mature supply chains.

The most urgent issue facing supply chains mainly serving mature products or services is the achievement of new product development. Whether the issue can be resolved successfully depends partly on how to use earned money from selling the present major products or services for succeeding in new product development. The problem will be explored in another chapter in the book.

References

Abernathy, W. J. and Utterback, J. M. (1978). Patterns of Industrial Innovation, *Technology Review*, Vol. 80, No. 7, pp. 40–47.

Bouillon, M. L., Ferrier, G. D., Stuebs Jr., M. T., and West, T. D. (2006). The Economic Benefit of Goal Congruence and Implications for Management Control Systems, *Journal of Accounting and Public Policy*, Vol. 25, No. 3, pp. 265–298.

Clark, K. B. (1985). The Interaction of Design Hierarchies and Market Concepts in Technological Evolution, *Research Policy*, Vol. 14, No. 5, pp. 235–251.

Demmy, S. and Talbott, J. (1998). Improve Internal Reporting with ABC and TOC, *Management Accounting*, November, pp. 18–24.

Dugdale, D. and Jones, T. C. (1998). Throughput Accounting: Transforming Practices? *British Accounting Review*, Vol. 30, No. 3, pp. 203–220.

Galloway, D. and Waldron, D. (1988a). Throughput Accounting — Part 1: The Need for a New Language for Manufacturing, *Management Accounting*, November, pp. 34–35.

Galloway, D. and Waldron, D. (1988b). Throughput Accounting — Part 2: Ranking Products Profitably, *Management Accounting*, December, pp. 34–35.

Galloway, D. and Waldron, D. (1989a). Throughput Accounting — Part 3: A Better Way to Control Labour Costs, *Management Accounting*, January, pp. 32–33.

Galloway, D. and Waldron, D. (1989b). Throughput Accounting — Part 4: Moving on to Complex Products, *Management Accounting*, February, pp. 40–41.

Hedley, B. (1977). Strategy and the "Business Portfolio", *Long Range Planning*, Vol. 10, No. 1, pp. 9–15.

Kilger, C. (2000). Definition of a Supply Chain Project, in *Supply Chain Management and Advanced Planning*, edited by Stadtler, H. and Kilger, C., Berlin: Springer, pp. 197–216.

Lambert, D. M., Emmelhainz, J. T., and Gardner, J. T. (1996). Developing and Implementing Supply Chain Partnerships, *The International Journal of Logistics Management*, Vol. 7, No. 2, pp. 1–18.

Macdivitt, H. and Wilkinson, M. (2012). *Value-Based Pricing: Drive Sales and Boost Your Bottom Line by Creating, Communicating, and Capturing Customer Value*, New York: The McGraw-Hill Companies.

Woodside, A. G., Golfetto, F., and Gibbert, M. (2008). Customer Value: Theory, Research, and Practice, in *Creating and Managing Superior Customer Value*, edited by Woodside, A. G., Golfetto, F., and Gibbert, M., Greenwich, Conn.: JAI Press, pp. 3–25.

Chapter 8

Cost Management in Supply Chains from a Life Cycle Perspective

1. Introduction

In recent years, many global markets have experienced increased volatility in the demand for finished goods. This situation has highlighted the challenges that firms face in swiftly responding to fluctuations in consumer demand for such goods. Supply chains can enable their participants to overcome such challenges effectively and efficiently. They provide intrinsic strategic value by creating partnership frameworks, and, by facilitating sharing of information on competitive factors such as consumer demand. In this way, supply chains enable firms to optimize consumer satisfaction; thus the ability to participate in well-integrated and highly cooperative supply chains provides firms with a competitive edge. All firms, irrespective of whether they are engaged in upstream, midstream, or downstream operations, face the managerial challenge of maintaining a competitive edge. Hence, being part of an effective and efficient supply chain has become a core strategy for sustainable corporate development, a situation that has led to intensified competition among supply chains (Minagawa, 2014).

According to Cäker and Strömsten (2010), when considering the most appropriate solutions to interorganizational management issues, business practitioners and academic researchers should aim for consumer satisfaction. The rule of thumb, when deciding on which practice to use in supply chain management is, to choose the one that consumers will value the most.

The stage of the life cycle of a product has an impact on consumer demand for the product or service. Consequently, consumer demand for a product at the growth stage differs from consumer demand for the product at the maturity stage. This study explores effective supply chain strategies across key stages of a product's life cycle.

The technologies embedded in products that are developing are found at the introductory and growth stages of products' technological life cycles: they offer significant potential for extensive and radical product innovation (Utterback and Abernathy, 1975; Abernathy and Clark, 1985). These characteristics of growing products facilitate frequent and rapid new product releases by a firm. Led partly by the expansion of product innovation on the supply side, consumers are increasingly demanding newer innovative products from firms. Meanwhile, mature products, which are at the maturity stages of their technological life cycles, offer low potential for product innovation. Consumers in mature product markets tend to value "efficient and effective purchases" more highly when selecting mature products, a scenario that will be explained here in further detail. Based on this perspective of supply chain management, the current study makes a distinction between supply chains that market growth products and those that market mature products. The purpose of the study is to examine, based on a review of relevant literature, theoretically and logically relevant cost management systems in inter-firm networks. This study also addresses the issue of control of supply chains that consist of independent firms, in which all partners are engaged in long-term implementation of supply chain operations. Supply chain development through exchange partners is not part of this chapter's research framework.

2. Review of Related Literature

2.1. Cost management that suits the characteristics of products offered by supply chains

Fisher (1997) proposes a research framework for examining supply chains' management control systems that suit the characteristics of their products.

He categorizes products as functional or innovative (Fisher, 1997). This approach regards a functional product as one that is widely distributed, relatively inexpensive, and frequently purchased. To increase the profitability of functional products, cost-minimization is of essence. In contrast, innovative products are considered identical to the growing products described in Section 1. Once supply chains that provide innovative products fail to market new and emerging products, they are no longer able to compete with other supply chains.

2.2. Customer accounting that fosters increases in customer value

Lind and Wedin (2005), and Lind and Strömsten (2006) present two research frameworks for supply chains. The first concerns the four basic types of customer relationships, in terms of a relationship matrix of customer and product traits. The second addresses the conceptualized customer accounting systems for particular customer relationships. In the conceptualization of customer accounting, products are divided into two categories; namely, growing products that are at the introductory and growth stages and thus meet new customer demand, and mature products that are produced in accordance with predetermined and standardized specifications. Customers have been classified as heavy and light purchasers.

The conceptual categorization of customer accounting proposed by Lind and Wedin (2005), and Lind and Strömsten (2006), is based on the following two fundamental considerations with regard to customer information that firms require. First, firms that market growing products must gain information related to expected returns on future investments in these products, since market demand is expected to increase over time. On the other hand, firms that supply mature products seek out information about profitability, and returns from sale of products, to individual customers during a specified period. Second, firms that manage relationships with light purchasers need information gained through segmental profitability analysis.

Lind and Wedin (2005), and Lind and Strömsten (2006), also describe four types of customer-accounting and the information required for each. The first type of customer-accounting is the management of relationships with light purchasers in mature product markets. This requires information from segmental profitability analysis, based on groups of customers who possess common characteristics.

The second type of customer-accounting is the management of relationships with heavy purchasers in mature product markets. For this, we require information on current profitability of individual customers.

The third type of customer-accounting is the management of relationships with heavy purchasers in growing product markets. This type requires information from the analysis of customer-lifetime-value. Customer-lifetime-value is a measure of the potential for future continuity of an existing relationship with a customer. It is generally calculated as the sum of cumulative discounted cash flows that customer of a firm generates in sales over the duration of his or her association with the firm (lifetime).

According to Ryals (2008, pp. 83–102), there are four steps to the calculation of customer-lifetime-value. The first is forecasting a customer's lifetime in years. The second is forecasting annual revenue generated by the customer over the remaining lifetime of the relationship. The third is forecasting the annual matching costs, namely, the product cost, and the cost to serve (CTS) customers (see Section 3), alongside the revenue calculated in the second step. The fourth is calculating the net present value of the future net cash flows generated by the customer. Thus, the maximization of customer lifetime value requires a firm to increase revenue while reducing costs including the CTS customers.

The fourth type of customer accounting is the management of relationships with lead users of a growing product, where bulk purchases are not made. This type of accounting requires information from customer equity analysis. Customer equity is the total lifetime value of a group of customers.

3. Achieving Growth in Supply Chains Through Cost Management

This study distinguishes between supply chains that market growing products, and inter-firm networks that supply mature products. It then identifies consumer demand for finished products of these two types of supply chains. The research framework of the study makes it possible to examine the types of cost management that are required to satisfy consumers in both instances.

3.1. Supply chains that market growing products

3.1.1. *Consumer Needs for Growing Products*

Growing products are at the growth stage of the technology life cycle, where there is significant potential for product innovation. Continuous product innovation on the supply side raises the market demand for release of new products. Growing products can thus facilitate product technology breakthroughs. At the same time, markets for growing products constantly increase their demand for new products, making it impossible for firms to survive, unless they continue to innovate. This competitive environment calls an inevitable increase in capital investment. Firms in growing product markets, therefore, face the challenge of raising sufficient funds to survive product innovation races. One source of funds that can be used to finance such investments is the "cash cow" of product portfolio management (PPM) (Hedley, 1977).

More importantly, the ability to generate profits swiftly through marketing and sale of growing products has a positive effect on the establishment of sustainable competitive advantages. This ability is taken into account in this study's research perspective.

3.1.2. *Life-Cycle Cost Analysis*

The essence of competitive strategies in markets for growing products lies in finding ways to fully satisfy consumers effectively and efficiently by enabling rapid acquisition of new products. Thus, capital investment in the development and supply of new products is crucial to sustaining a supply chain's competitive advantage over others. Constantly changing market environments also force supply chain participants to accelerate time-to-market (TTM) for new products at low costs, in order to gain crucial competitive advantages. The concept of break-even time (BET), which Hewlett-Packard utilized for new product development, is an

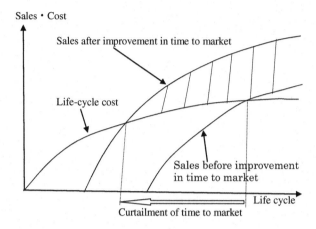

Figure 8.1.   The impact of reducing time to market on life-cycle profit

Note: The area marked by the diagonal lines shows the incremental increase in sales generated by a reduction in the time to market without increasing the life-cycle cost.

effective performance metric for managerially auditing the achievement of agile TTM. BET is defined as the amount of time taken to recoup total investment expenditure. The longer the BET, the riskier an investment will be; it will take a longer period for the investor to recoup the invested capital on the basis of discounted cash flows (House and Price, 1991).

In Figure 8.1, the BET is represented by the point where the sales line and the life-cycle cost (see Figure 8.2) for a certain product intersect. The life-cycle cost of a product consists, as shown in Figure 8.2, of the costs incurred by the product's supply chain partners and the product's user cost. Customers pay for a product's usage and disposal costs in the latter stages of the product's life cycle. Supply chains must reduce customers' usage and disposal costs, thereby increasing sales and enhancing customer satisfaction. If it is assumed that the first developer of a new product will exclusively monopolize demand, the acceleration of TTM can cause a rise in the gradient of the sales line as shown in Figure 8.1. Effective cost management enables the acceleration of TTM-driven revenue improvement, thereby yielding a reduction in the BET.

According to Clark and Fujimoto (1991), the best practices for reducing TTM include concerted efforts at product development, and joint research and development (R&D) between upstream and downstream firms. The most important challenge in R&D, is the optimization of

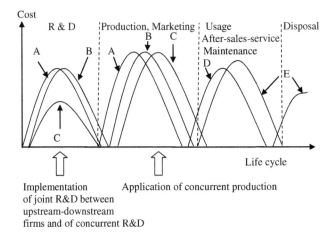

Figure 8.2.   Conceptualization of supply chain life-cycle costing

Notes:

1. A: Parts manufacturers, B: Finished product manufacturers, C: Marketing firms, D: Manufacturing industries, E: Consumers.

2. Joint R&D and concurrent production are based on Fujimoto (2001).

time-cost trade-off (Cohen *et al.*, 1996). Unless firms can succeed in reducing both TTM- and R&D-related costs, they cannot improve their profitability. Moreover, the acceleration of projects tends to need additional resource consumption, thereby increasing costs. Solving the time-cost problem for new product development, calls for life-cycle cost analysis.

3.1.3.   *Design to Life-Cycle Cost*

Life-cycle costing tracks and accumulates the cost attributable to a product, right from the initial stage of R&D to the product's disposal (Horngren *et al.*, 1994, p. 443). Life-cycle costs for a product comprise the costs incurred by the product's suppliers, namely, the costs incurred by firms responsible for R&D, product design, production, and marketing, and the product's user costs, which include usage and disposal costs. One reason why managers emphasize life-cycle costing is because the cost incurred on a product's design process at the early stages of the product's life cycle influences the actual costs incurred at the later stages. These later costs are production costs, the CTS and support customers, usage costs, and disposal cost. The earlier cost has an influence on the later costs because a product's design substantially affects the product's function, its quality, methods for manufacturing and delivering the product, its usage, and the method for disposal. Thus, a product's design affects not only the actual costs incurred during the later operations of the product's suppliers, but also the cost incurred by the product's users. In life-cycle cost management, the focus is optimizing the trade-off between the actual cost of a product's design, and the costs incurred by later operations of the product's suppliers. Moreover, increasing the costs of a product's suppliers tends to contribute to reducing the costs incurred by the product's users.

According to Wang *et al.* (2007), redesign-driven changes to a product's parts, contribute to a reduction in the product's life-cycle costs by changing various operations at different stages of the overall production process. Specifically, changes made to parts can change the design process, production methods, parts procurement, and disposal methods, thereby reducing R&D, production, part procurement, and product disposal costs, respectively (Wang *et al.*, 2007).

The most useful method to optimize total cost of ownership for best value growing products is design to life-cycle cost. This product-design engineering technique aims at attaining design for manufacturability to reduce manufacturing costs across the supply chain as well as design for easy and economical use and disposal of the product to reduce user costs.

3.1.4. *Synergy of Life-Cycle Costing and Activity-Based Costing*

Combining life-cycle costing and activity-based costing can generate activity-based cost data and cost data driven by resource-consumption for operations at the various stages of a product's life cycle (Dunk, 2004, p. 404). The combination of the two costing systems reveals relations among the quantities of resources consumed in various operational activities in a product's entire life cycle, thereby making it possible to calculate how changes in the costs of activities at a certain stage of the product's life cycle, affect the costs of correlated activities.

The most critical factor in the success of supply chains that offer fast-growing products is the swift marketing of new products. The degree of managerial success in this respect, can be evaluated using the performance levels of the BETs for new products. BET is calculated as the elapsed time between the moment of initial spending on the development of a product and the moment when net operating profit equals the total cost of design and development. Supply chains that market fast-growing products at the growth stage of a product's life cycle, should determine a BET target for a new product, and then consider whether the life-cycle cost target is achievable for the chosen BET. Life-cycle costs are broken down in terms of the participants responsible for operations across a supply chain (see Figure 8.2). This means that individual supply chain participants can be made responsible for the achievement of time and cost targets for their assigned operations. Thus, supply chain partners must determine ways to achieve target times and costs for their operations.

Life-cycle costing shows that decision-making related to operations at the early stages of a life cycle, affects the efficiency of operations at the later stages. Thus, all partners must cooperate and develop a supply chain's operations, in order to achieve results at the optimal time and cost.

Based on the aforementioned approach, activity-based life-cycle costing (ABLCC) can be regarded as an integrated system of life-cycle costing, and activity-based costing that provides firms with cutting-edge management practice (Emblemsvåg, 2003). ABLCC is a characteristic of a process-oriented method (Emblemsvåg, 2003). It breaks up a product's life cycle into a chain of activities and, then applies activity-based costing to each stage. Consequently, ABLCC across a supply chain can calculate how activities at an upstream firm affect the cost at an activity-driven downstream firm, and how activities within the supply chain affect the activity-driven costs of end users. This can be understood from the simple illustration below (Figure 8.3). Figure 8.3 demonstrates that consumer needs trigger activities across the supply chain. Specifically, a consumer's activities affect the activity-based cost driver's consumption quantity at the downstream firm, thereby generating its activity cost. Next, the quality and quantity of the activities at the downstream firm affects the actual activity-based cost of the upstream firm.

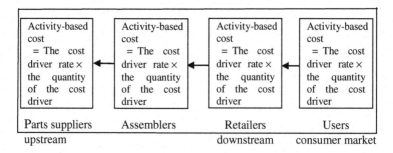

Figure 8.3. Consumer needs trigger the activity-based costs of the supply chain's partners

Note: Arrows show the effects of the upstream firms' activities on the downstream firms' activity-driven costs.

Furthermore, ABLCC can make operational activities conducted by supply chain participants manageable. Meeting the cost target over a product's life-cycle period requires optimal decision-making about the activities that must be executed, how they are to be performed them, and how inter-participant interface activities must be carried out. These issues can be solved optimally through the application of ABLCC.

3.1.5. *The Allocation of Supply Chains' Joint Profits Among Participants*

Supply chains must establish an effective incentive system to facilitate reaching an optimal trade-off between TTM and supply chain costs (see Figure 8.1). Otherwise, it will be impossible to increase supply chains' profits. Operational effectiveness and efficiency at early stages of a life cycle influence operational performance at the later life-cycle stages. Thus, the most important factor for the maximization of supply chains' joint profits is enhanced cooperation among participants. Therefore, the allocation of a supply chain's joint profits among its participants is an essential incentive to improve partnerships among suppliers. This study sheds light on what rule is to be used for the allocation of such profits to individual participants in proportion to the ratio of total costs borne by them. Joint profits across supply chains are calculated as follows:

$$X = a - b - c,$$

where X is a supply chain's joint profit from a finished products, a is the turnover of the finished product, b is the supply chain's total variable cost for the finished product, excluding those incurred through internal purchases within the supply chain, and c is the supply chain's total capacity cost for the finished product. The capacity-related cost for a firm is the cost that is associated with human capital and productive facilities; moreover, the cost is incurred as a result of possessing these facilities and preparing them to be usable at any time.

The allocation of a supply chain's joint profit based on the individual participant's costs results in equal profit per unit of cost across participants (Dudek, 2003, p. 134). This method of joint profit distribution, based on cost incurred, is fair.

3.2. Supply chains that market mature, standardized goods

3.2.1. *Lean Consumption (Womack and Jones, 2005)*

Products that are standardized because they have reached maturity in their product life cycles can be said to be at the maturity stage of their technology life cycles. Once products reach the maturity stage, new product development is no longer the most critical factor for profitability. The most important factor for supply chains distributing mature products is the convenience of purchase for customers.

Womack and Jones' (2005) lean consumption approach, which involves the optimization of purchase processes, applies the concept of purchase convenience as an analytical instrument. According to Womack and Jones (2005), firms need to follow six principles to achieve lean consumption. The first principle is that firms need to completely solve any problems that consumers face by ensuring goods and services offered are working (p. 61). The second requirement is to help and promote valuable utilization of consumer time by excluding non-value-added time from the precious total time that consumers can spare (p. 62). The third requirement is to provide the exact goods that consumers demand. Firms should not struggle to distribute what they want to sell to consumers; rather they need to strive to satisfy market demand, by offering precisely what consumers want (p. 63). The fourth requirement is to satisfy consumers by providing what they want exactly where they want it. In order to meet consumers' needs better, it is important to segment consumers into smaller groups, according to the places or stores where they make purchases, and then construct distribution channels for these stores. This approach enables consumers to obtain what they want, where they want. This will lead to higher revenues for retailers (pp. 66–67). The fifth requirement is to provide the right consumers with the right items in the right stores at exactly the right time (p. 67). The sixth requirement adds further value to existing goods, thereby satisfying rapidly expanding consumer demand. If the various demands of consumers can be met with goods offered by a single firm, it can save them a significant amount of time and the hassle of transacting with many firms (p. 68).

3.2.2. *The CTS Customers*

In mature markets, consumers barely perceive the functional differentiation among goods of different firms. Instead, the second to fifth principles of the lean consumption approach of Womack and Jones (2005) described in Section 3.2.1 affect consumers' purchase decisions more strongly. In other words, one of the most important factors for achieving competitiveness in the sale of mature goods is the ability to provide, swiftly and conveniently, what consumers want at low prices.

In this respect, the most important issue facing supply chains is the challenge of improving convenience of consumer purchase without increasing costs. Standardized goods that have passed through the growth periods of their product life cycles face difficulty in earning large revenues if they remain as they are. Thus, supply chains that provide mature goods must reduce costs, otherwise, they cannot increase their profits.

It is essential for supply chains that are devoted to providing mature goods to have a better understanding of the types of purchase assistance that consumers want and need. Based on information from marketing, supply chains must also decide what purchase assistance to offer to their segmented consumer base and how to provide it. However, supply chains that serve mature goods must reduce CTS customers, since market conditions make it difficult to increase sales.

The CTS customers is instrumental in making decisions based on customer profitability analysis (Shapiro *et al.*, 1987; Braithwaite and Samakh, 1998; Guerreiro *et al.*, 2008). The CTS customers is also useful in analyzing marketing costs based on product-segmentation in activity-based costing involving contribution margin analysis, as proposed by Monden (2001). This type of analysis integrates activity-based costing with contribution margin analysis to achieve more accurate stage-by-stage recovery of fixed costs, thereby enabling more useful customer profitability management. Further, Shapiro *et al.* (1987) classify the CTS customers into three categories: the cost of obtaining an order entry activity, the cost of production, and the cost of delivery.

Consumers' purchase choices for standardized goods are significantly affected by supply chains' quality of customer service. Here, customer service includes purchasing assistance, quick delivery, and after-sales service. Because this study examines the impact of the CTS customers on the improvement of how customers value mature products, we consider the different types of CTS, except production-related cost. According to Guerreiro *et al.* (2008, p. 392), diverse terms have been used interchangeably to describe CTS, such as "customer service cost" in the work of Hansen and Mowen (2000), "marketing cost" in Foster and Gupta (1994), and "marketing and logistics cost" in Stapleton *et al.* (2004). The current study uses the CTS customers as a term to describe the cost concept of CTS.

Management practices based on the CTS customers identify cost drivers for marketing activities and activities that support consumer purchase based on activity-based costing. Such activities include successful order placements, distribution, and after-sales-services. Analysis of these drivers will enable informed decisions based on how much it will cost to provide customer with the services they want.

Figure 8.4 shows the importance of the analysis of CTS customers by using the marketing cost approach of Coughlan *et al.* (2006). Marketing activity costs include costs incurred for storage and logistics, carrying inventories, winning orders, negotiations, proceeds collection, receiving and placing orders, and payments, as well as cost-related to compensation, and repairs and after-sales service.

CTS customers determines cost drivers, which in turn determine quality and quantity standards for different types of customer service

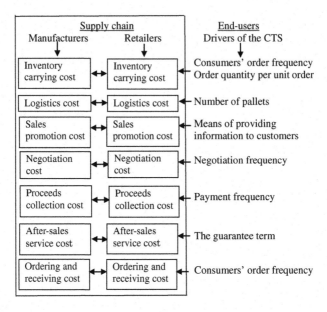

Figure 8.4.   Illustration of costs of providing services to customers

Note: The categorization of customer service activities is based on Couglan *et al.* (2006, p. 74).

activities provided by firms to their customers. This capability of cost drivers can lead to the generation of cost functions for customer service activities. For example, if inventory-carrying cost is proportionate to order-placing frequency, the inventory-carrying cost for each order placed can be estimated.

3.2.3. *Managerial Effectiveness of the CTS Customers*

(1) The determination of activities that achieve effective customer service efficiently

Many industries today are faced with shortening product life cycles. Under such market conditions, sales will inevitably decline. The shorter a product's life cycle, the greater the challenge of reducing its operational cost. Crucial to cost reduction for supply chains that provide mature goods is the achievement of "efficient" purchasing by consumers. To achieve "efficient" purchasing, the cost of serving customers needs to be borne in mind.

A strategy for boosting sales of mature goods can be to market a wide variety of such goods. In theory, manufacturing and marketing a wide variety of production, can respond to diverse consumer demands, thereby leading to an increase in sales. However, it has been seen that it is almost impossible to increase the sales of mature goods; thus, to increase profitability, supply chains of mature goods must reduce the cost of serve.

When choosing among mature goods offered by different supply chains, consumers give greater importance to the quality of purchase assistance provided by firms than to the functionality of goods. Moreover, increasing the variety of products offered inevitably increases the CTS customers. Thus, efficient serving of customers is the most decisive factor in increasing the sales of mature goods. A consequent managerial analysis of the CTS customers can be broken down into two stages: forming a better understanding about the content and quality of purchase assistance that customers need, followed by an estimation of the cost incurred on offering the service to customers.

Another business strategy for supply chains that market mature goods, is selecting a few core goods, and building core competence around them. Selecting a few core goods requires a more detailed analysis of customer profitability. Activity-based costing traces CTS directly to customers as a costing objective by using activity cost drivers. Kaplan and Anderson (2004, 2007) present the effectiveness of time-based activity cost drivers. The example of customer service activities and their cost drivers is as follows. Distribution costs are affected by the time required, and the quantity and weight of stock keeping unit (SKU) transported. Warehousing costs are affected by the stock days, and the quantity and weight of pallets handled. Billing costs are affected by the time required and the quantity of bills issued. Sales costs are affected the time required. Sales promotion costs are affected by the time and type of promotion. Merchandising costs are affected by commercial contracts. Collecting costs are affected by the time required (Guerreiro *et al.*, 2008). The CTS customers, using activity-based costing, is instrumental in allocating marketing-activity-related overhead to customer segments correctly.

(2) The shiftability of marketing activities among supply chain participants

Bringing about an improvement in effectiveness and efficiency, in the purchasing behavior of consumers requires supply chain participants, such as parts' manufacturers, manufacturers of finished products, and retailers, to consider strategies to fundamental restructure the ways by which to provide consumers with goods. An effective management technique for this is functional shiftability. Supply chains must achieve customer satisfaction efficiently by identifying the best performers of individual functions in a supply chain, and then allocating the functions to partners best suited for each function. This is the role of functional shiftability (Mallen, 1973). This, though, is more feasible and effective in trust-based, well-integrated supply chains than in arm's length transactions.

Functional shiftability can help to save time when goods must be transported to customers. However, functional shiftability in supply chains is likely to cause an increase in the operational costs of those participants that must engage in new tasks transferred from other participants. The focal firm of a supply chain must, therefore, create some incentive for participants to accept functional shiftability in spite of the increase in costs. Among the incentives is the allocation of joint profit among participants across the supply chain.

4. Concluding Remarks

Almost all goods have recently experienced shrinking life cycles, and drastic changes in consumer demand. The challenge of the changing market can be successfully addressed by supply chains. Since they naturally excel in quick dissemination of market- and management-related information among their participants, supply chains enable swift delivery of goods to consumers according to their demands. Growth and profitability of individual firms depend largely on whether or not they can be part of a well-integrated and highly competitive supply chain. This competitive requirement applies to all firms across the supply chain. As the competition among supply chains continues to intensify, the focal participants in a supply chain will need to continuously introduce advanced managerial practices across the supply chain. In this context, the current study has examined supply chain cost management.

References

Abernathy, W. J. and Clark, K. B. (1985). Innovation: Mapping the Winds of Creative Destruction, *Research Policy*, Vol. 14, No. 1, pp. 3–22.

Braithwaite, A. and Samakh, E. (1998). The Cost-To-Serve Method, *International Journal of Logistics Management*, Vol. 9, No. 1, pp. 69–84.

Cäker, M. and Strömsten, T. (2010). Customer Accounting When Relationships and Networks Matter, in *Accounting in Networks*, edited by Håkansson, H., Kraus, K., and Lind, J., London: Routledge, pp. 151–183.

Cohen, M. A., Eliashberg, J., and Teck-Hua Ho (1996). New Product Development: The Performance and Time-to-Market Tradeoff, *Management Science*, Vol. 42, No. 2, pp. 173–186.

Coughlan, A. T., Anderson, E., Stern, L. W., and EI-Ansary, A. I. (2006). *Marketing Channels* (7th Edition), New Jersey: Prentice Hall.

Clark, K. and Fujimoto, T. (1991). *Product Development Performance: Strategy, Organization, and Management in the World Auto Industry*, Boston: Harvard University Press.

Dudek, G. (2003). *Collaborative Planning in Supply Chains*, Berlin: Springer.

Dunk, A. S. (2004). Product Life Cycle Cost Analysis: The Impact of Customer Profiling, Competitive Advantage, and Quality of IS Information, *Management Accounting Research*, Vol. 15, No. 4, pp. 401–414.

Emblemsvåg, J. (2003). *Life-Cycle Costing: Using Activity-Based Costing and Monte Carlo Methods to Manage Future Costs and Risks*, New Jersey: John Wiley & Sons.

Fisher, M. L. (1997). What is the Right Supply Chain for Your Product? *Harvard Business Review*, March–April, pp. 105–116.

Foster, G. and Gupta, M. (1994). Marketing, Cost Management and Management Accounting, *Journal of Management Accounting Research*, Vol. 6, pp. 43–77.

Fujimoto, T. (2001). *Introduction to Production Management*, Tokyo: Nihon Keizai Shimbun (in Japanese).

Guerreiro, R., Bio, S. R., and Merschmann, E. V. V. (2008). Cost-To-Serve Measurement and Customer Profitability Analysis, *International Journal of Logistics Management*, Vol. 19, No. 3, pp. 389–407.

Hansen, D. R. and Mowen, M. M. (2000). *Cost Management: Accounting and Control* (3rd Edition), Nashville: South-Western College Publishing.

Hedley, B. (1977). Strategy and the "Business Portfolio", *Long Range Planning*, Vol. 10, pp. 9–15.

Horngren, C. T., Datar, S. M., and Foster, G. (1994). Cost Accounting: A Managerial Emphasis (8th Edition), New Jersey: Prentice Hall.

House, C. H. and Price, R. L. (1991). The Return Map: Tracking Product Teams, *Harvard Business Review*, January–February, pp. 92–101.

Kaplan, R. S. and Anderson, S. R. (2004). Time-driven Activity Based Costing, *Harvard Business Review*, Vol. 82, No. 11, pp. 131–138.

Kaplan, R. S. and Anderson, S. R. (2007). *Time-driven Activity Based Costing: A Simpler and More Powerful Path to Higher Profits*, Boston: Harvard Business School Press.

Lind, J. and Strömsten, T. (2006). When Do Firms Use Different Types of Customer Accounting? *Journal of Business Research*, Vol. 59, No. 12, pp. 1257–1266.

Lind, J. and Wedin, T. (2005). *Interorganizational Resource Interfaces and the Use of Customer Accounting*, The 21st IMP conference in Rotterdam, The Netherlands.

Mallen, B. (1973). Functional Spin-Off: A Key to Anticipating Change in Distribution Structure, *Journal of Marketing*, Vol. 37, No. 3, pp. 18–25.

Minagawa, Y. (2014). Supply Chains Cost Management: A Life Cycle Perspective, *Journal of Nagoya Gakuin University; Social Sciences*, Vol. 51, No. 1, pp. 1–14.

Monden, Y. (2001). *Management Accounting*, Tokyo: Zeimu keiri kyokai (in Japanese).

Ryals, L. (2008). *Managing Customer Profitability*, England: John Wiley & Sons.

Shapiro, B. P., Rangan, V. K., Moriarty, R. T., and Ross, E. B. (1987). Manage Customers for Profits (Not Just for Sales), *Harvard Business Review*, September–October, pp. 101–108.

Stapleton, D., Sangamitra, P., Beach, E., and Julmanichoti, P. (2004). Activity Based Costing for Logistics and Marketing, *Business Process Management Journal*, Vol. 10, No. 5, pp. 584–597.

Utterback, J. M. and Abernathy, W. J. (1975). A Dynamic Model of Product and Process Innovation, *Omega*, Vol. 3, No. 6, pp. 639–656.

Wang, L., Bing, S., Xiang, L., and Ng, W. K. (2007). *A Product Family Based Life Cycle Cost Model for Part Variety and Change Analysis*, International Conference on Engineering Design 2007 [online], Paris, August, 28–31. Available at: http://www.designsociety.org/download-publication/25377/ [Accessed June 15, 2018].

Womack, J. P. and Jones, D. T. (2005). Lean Consumption, *Harvard Business Review*, March, pp. 58–68.

Chapter 9

Supply Chain Quality Management

1. Introduction

Let us suppose that some fabricated defectives were not detected by a component manufacturing participant in a supply chain, and were delivered to an assembling participant. The assembling participant also did not completely identify these defectives and ended up serving defective products to consumers, who claimed liability for the defective products. The worst scenario shows that misidentification of defects within the supply chain results in lost trust and lost sales in the market, since consumers were hampered by defective products.

It is necessary to ensure zero product or service error at all stages of the overall process in a supply chain. This absolutely enables the improvement of the profitability of both the entire supply chain and its partners. The occurrence of defects in any participant in the supply chains results in a delay in time-to-consumer:time-to-market. That is, an error at any stage across the whole supply chain gives rise to prolonged time taken to deliver the correct product or service to the end-consumer. The achievement of zero-defect can prevent lost sales due to a delay in time-to-consumer caused by quality error(s). Therefore, it is useful to conduct and transmit the financial performance measurement regarding quality improvement for individual supply chain partners throughout the supply chain. This can facilitate the collaborative quality control of supply chains.

How can supply chains prevent serving of defective goods to consumers? This study explains the benefits of transparent open book oriented management control systems to avoid financial risk originating from poor quality. The aim of management control systems addressed in this study is to quantify the achievement degree of supply chain quality improvement and diffuse that across the overall supply chain. Quality affects the competitive advantage of both the entire supply chain and individual partners. Therefore, the sharing of financial information related to quality among supply chain partners can help motivate them to strive for collaborative supply chain quality improvement.

The study considers quality costing, which uses the degree of conformity to requirement or specification to quantify quality. Quality costs originate from the following two cost-drivers: quality control activities undertaken to secure conformity to targeted specification, and failure in the attainment of the conformity. Moreover, sharing information on the degree of inter-firm network-wide quality improvement with the members needs the establishment of supply chain traceability systems regarding goods flow. According to the US Food and Drug Administration, traceability is the ability to identify by means of paper or electronic records a food product and its producer, from where and when the product was sourced, and to where and when it was delivered (FAO, 2003).

Since the poor quality of products or services has negative consequences on the revenue of the overall supply chain and the participants, quality control in supply chain management was examined in many previous studies. For instance, Obied-Allah (2015) researched the impact of quality cost sharing and revenue sharing contracts on supply chain management.

Inspired by previous research, the study addresses how supply chains can achieve the highest quality of product or service. At the heart of the issue is to find a way to integrate quality control of each supply chain partner, each of which is a separate legal entity. The biggest challenge of supply chain quality control is that it requires that all the members of a supply chain devote themselves to making no quality errors. A proposed solution of the issue in the study is the formation and execution of strategies for improving the overall supply chain quality and opening quality performance to partners. Moreover, the study examines the advantages of allocating the joint profit of supply chains to the participants according to their cost.

The rest of this study is organized as follows. Section 2 describes the essence of the two concepts: quality cost and traceability. These can lead to the formulation of the framework of this research. Section 2 also explains the strategic values of quality cost and traceability based on literature review. Section 3 explains the benefits of product and process design engineering tools to prevent quality failure. Section 4 explores the effects of accelerating quality control based on the traceability system for competitive advantages. Section 5 examines the way to facilitate the supply chain-wide implementation of product and process design engineering, and the establishment of traceability systems through quality costing.

2. Literature Review

2.1. Strategic value of quality cost

Quality costing uses the degree of conformity to requirements or specifications so as to operationally measure quality. Quality differs from grade. A high grade product is one that has several features and benefits. A process to measure quality based on conformity to requirements starts from the specification of a targeted grade level. Among certain grade-level categorized products, some may have a higher conformity to specifications, while others may have lower conformity.

Quality costs originate from the following two causes. The first cause is the activity undertaken to ensure the conformity of products to target specifications. The quality costs involve both prevention and appraisal costs. Prevention costs arise from the removal of latent defects. Appraisal costs include the expenses for maintaining company quality levels by means of formal evaluation of quality of goods. This involves cost elements such as inspection, outside endorsement, and quality audits (Feigenbaum, 1961, p. 84).

The second cause is failure in the attainment of conformity. The inferior quality-driven costs consist of internal and external failure costs (Feigenbaum, 1961, pp. 88–89). These costs are caused by quality error(s). Internal failure costs are incurred before defective goods are shipped to customers. They involve scrap, reworking of defective units, and down-time caused by quality problems. If defective products are shipped to customers, external failure costs arise. External failure costs include reputational and contractual costs (Baiman *et al.*, 2000). Reputational costs are measured using lost sales because of loss of reputation caused by poor quality. Contractual costs involve recall-driven communication cost, warranties, fines, and lawsuits.

Nandakumar *et al.* (1993) propose that it is important to measure the cost of congestion and disruption in operations caused by quality problems as an item of internal failure costs. The costs of congestion and disruption are represented by the incremental carrying and holding costs of inventories (Nandakumar *et al.*, 1993, p. 5). Inventory carrying costs include: the opportunity cost of investment tied up in inventory (the expected financial return that capital invested in inventory could be expected to earn in an alternative investment of equivalent risk), inventory storage cost, inventory risk cost (obsolescence, damage, deterioration costs).

The reason for defect occurrence increasing the cost of congestion is discussed as follows. Failure to conform to specification requirements causes operation delay at several stages in factories, thereby resulting in longer waiting lines of work in progress at individual manufacturing processes for the next manufacturing process.

The promotion of capital investment for the prevention and inspection of quality activities can have substantial positive impact on the reduction of production errors, thereby contributing to reduced costs occurring due to poor quality. Therefore, firms need to determine the appropriate level of capital investment toward facilitating the prevention and inspection activities and ultimately maximizing profits. Thus, these managerial decisions require quality costing.

2.2. Strategic value of prevention costs

An essential challenge to quality management is to avoid errors from occurring at any stage while supplying high quality products or services to consumers at a higher cost-effectiveness ratio. To attain this objective, Beecroft (2003) observes that prevention costs need to be incurred for activities that ensure that errors are not made in the development, design, production, and shipping stages (Beecroft, 2003, p. 32). They include design costs of both product and manufacturing processes that can root out defect generating factors.

Product design and production process design that enable the achievement of excellent product quality are strategically valuable. Such effective design practices will be described in the later section.

Spending sufficient funds on prevention and appraisal activities usually brings about a reduction in defects, thereby reducing internal and external failure costs. Obied-Allah (2015) showed that more investment of money in preventing poor quality has a positive relationship with supply chain profit.

2.3. Traceability systems for achieving network-wide transparency

Traceability is the ability to identify what the goods are, from where and when they were sourced, and to where and when they were delivered using ICT-based records (FAO, 2003). Traceability systems provide the following information: (1) what is the product, and when, where, what quantity, and by whom the product was produced. (2) When, where, how much, and by whom the product was deposited. (3) When, where, by whom, to whom, and in what quantity the product was delivered (Corina, 2013, p. 295).

Traceability allows supply chains responsible for recalls to quickly identify consumers who bought recalled products, thereby enabling the supply chain to quickly notify the consumers of the recalls. Traceability can facilitate in reduction of time taken to respond to product recalls. Accelerating of response to recall can hold down the decrease of a firm's brand reputation and, hence, keep lost sales lower.

3. Quality Failure Prevention During the Product and Process Design Stage

Quality defects are caused by manufacturing failures in factories and inherent failures in product and production process design (Taguchi and

Clausing, 1990, p. 66). Quality defects cause internal and external failure costs. Thus, cost is driven from quality failure including inferior products design and manufacturing methods causing defectives. To reduce the quality failure costs, it is important to develop product design methods that can achieve high quality, enhanced reliability, and the best customer satisfaction. Furthermore, firms must develop effective production methods that can achieve conformity of products to specifications. There are two facets of product design toward quality improvement: designing quality into the product, referred to as "design for quality" (DFQ) and designing manufacturable products, referred to as "design for manufacturability" (DFM) (Flynn *et al.*, 1995; Handfield *et al.*, 1999; Kaynak, 2003). The objective of QFD and QFM is to design products of high quality and reliability that can be easily and economically manufactured.

Yamaki *et al.* (2007) presented design methods for creating products of high quality and reliability, such as practices for improvement of chassis strength and high shock absorption effects. They also indicated building "manufacture methods enabling defect prevention" into the drawings. The design methods involve reducing the number of components constituting a finished product, and building fabrication methods for the prevention of defects into the drawings (Yamaki *et al.*, 2007).

According to Hinckley (1997), a source of nonconformity to quality requirements is complexity. Therefore, product and production process design that can eliminate complexity contributes to reducing defects.

4. Traceability Driven Speedy Response to Quality Failure

Let us suppose that assembling participants in supply chains found defectives out of the incoming parts from component manufacturing participants. How long does it take for the assembling participants to acquire quality parts and complete the manufacture of quality products? Whether the assembling partners can reduce time to acquire quality parts depends on the availability of inter-firm network-wide production history based on traceability systems. If traceability systems are not introduced, even knowing who fabricated impaired parts is time-consuming.

By focusing on companies having traceability systems in place, the assembling partners can easily retrieve a manufacturer to place an order for quality goods. Thus, companies with traceability systems can achieve rework more quickly than those without.

The accelerated fixing of defects within supply chains boosts the sales of finished products, because the delayed delivery of quality goods to consumers caused by poor quality can be eliminated through prompt responses to consumers.

Moreover, traceability systems contribute to an agile response to recalls in markets. Those companies that notified a recall for defective products in markets are obligated to remove or repair them. The more promptly product recall handling for each owner of the defective product is implemented, the smaller the degree of decrease in sales due to loss of reputation. Quick recall handling needs the quick identification of who purchased recalled products, and where they reside. Such requirements can be met by product purchaser traceability systems.

5. How to Facilitate Supply Chain-Wide Collaborative Quality Improvement

Two administrative tools facilitate quality improvement across the overall supply chain. The first tool is the conclusion of a contract wherein supply chain partners agree to be penalized if they fail to conform to specifications. The second tool is to inspire supply chain partners to work together toward the achievement of excellent quality. An effective method of motivating partners to cooperate and offer perfect finished goods to the customer is to make them recognize the importance of delivering quality goods for their own growth. Firms participate in supply chains in the expectation of boosting their profitability. The realization of the partners' competitive aspirations can enhance integration and cooperation among supply chain participants (Cowan *et al.*, 2015, pp. 141–142).

Of the above two tools for promoting supply chain quality improvement, this study addresses the latter: noncontractual, rather partners' autonomous-behavior-driven methods. The following discussion aims at examining methods that measure benefits enjoyed by partners through DFQ, DFM, and traceability.

5.1. Benefits of DFQ and DFM

An aim of DFQ is to prevent nonconformity to specifications during the product design stage. Expenses spent on DFQ are an item of prevention costs. A return from prevention costs is the removal of the causes of defects. Seen through the lens of quality costing, the incurrence of prevention costs can give rise to the prevention of quality failure of the supply chain, thereby yielding reductions in rework costs and congestion costs. Thus, these are the financial benefits of quality failure prevention. Moreover, prevention costs can reduce lost sales and recall costs. These losses are incurred by a damaged brand image caused by delivering defectives to customers in markets. Rework costs and congestion costs are categorized as internal failure costs. The loss of sales and recall costs are the elements of external failure costs.

The main aim of DFM is product design that can overcome difficulty in achieving error-free manufacturing effectively and efficiently. An engineering technique for DFM is the reduction of the number of parts in the product. A decrease in the total number of parts can reduce the difficulty of manufacturing an item, thereby making it error-free during its production (Yamaki *et al.*, 2007). As a result, decreases in internal and external failure costs can be attained.

Figure 9.1 shows whole life-cycle benefits created by product and process design engineering enabling error prevention. Prevention costs incurred by DFQ and DFM contribute to a decrease in internal failure costs such as those to fix poor quality during manufacturing within a supply chain. Moreover, both DFQ and DFM, commonly having the characteristics of zero-defect generating preventive design tools, can decrease defectives and manufacturing errors and avoid shipping defectives to consumers in markets. Thus, DFQ and DFM contribute to freeing from damaging the consumer and occurring product recalls, thereby increasing cash inflows through reducing the loss of sales after product launch.

Furthermore, Figure 9.1 shows what benefits supply chains can get and how much they can earn in return for prevention costs incurred by their partners. Through impressing all the partners of supply chains with

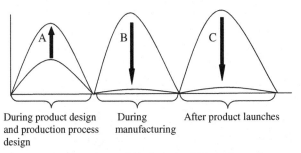

During product design   During   After product launches
and production process   manufacturing
design

A: Incremental costs incurred for designing high-quality products
   and effective production processes
B: Decreased internal failure costs due to design for high-quality and
   DFM
C: Decreased external failure costs

Figure 9.1.   Conceptualization of benefits of prevention costs

Note: The actual amount of costs incurred for design for high-quality and DFM depends on how effective firms can execute design engineering.

the importance of preventing poor quality of a product or service, the motivation of the partners toward engaging in collaborative supply chain quality improvement can be enhanced.

Therefore, the entire life-cycle-wide financial effects of DFQ and DFM are conceptualized as follows (see Figure 9.1). (1) During product design and manufacturing process design stages, incremental prevention costs were incurred by designing high-quality products and effective production processes using both DFQ and DFM. (2) Spending money on prevention activities, DFQ and DFM can reduce manufacturing error, thereby reducing internal failure costs. Why this is attainable is explained as follows. Since product design decides the mechanical traits of products and production methods, the amount of costs that will be incurred during the production stage is locked in during the design phase. Thus, cost improvement activities in the design stage have the most effective impact on cost reduction. (3) After the introduction of a new finished product, DFQ and DFM contribute toward avoiding delivery of defective products to the customer. As a result, decreases in external failure costs are achievable. An optimal level of spending on DFQ and DFM depends on how such design engineering concepts are executed.

5.2. How to effectively implement DFQ and DFM in supply chains

An issue which supply chains should overcome for achieving zero defects through DFQ and DFM is how to integrate expertise of its participants including marketers, component manufacturers, assemblers, and distributers into high quality assurance. Therefore, supply chains need to establish managerial practices to promote the integration of partners' expertise on product and production process design engineering into zero defect assurance.

A key success factor behind a higher competitive advantage of supply chains is the higher quality of overall supply chains. The quality level of the whole supply chain in turn is determined decisively by its individual participants' quality performance. Therefore, supply chain partners must invest their managerial resources in quality enhancement during the stage of product and production process design. The creation of product design which enables the achievement of the highest customer value needs integrated collaboration among supply chain partners. Network-wide sharing information regarding the overall supply chain financial performance related to DFQ and DFM is significantly conducive to motivate participants to devote their managerial resources to the design engineering practices. A financial measure for the performance of product and production process design is the reduction of internal and external quality failure costs as shown in Figure 9.1.

5.3. Traceability advantage

The slower the response to defects, the longer it takes to complete the fixing of defects. Consequently, the longer the delay of responses to defective products, the longer the time required to deliver quality products to customers. Longer time taken to reach target customers in the markets causes larger lost sales in markets. Therefore, speeding up response to defectives for preventing the occurrence of the delay of delivery time can more largely reduce the loss of sales in comparison with the case of slow responses to defectives caused by the unavailability of traceability systems.

Traceability systems concerning products and components in the supply chains contribute significantly to the achievement of accelerating the speed of responses to defective products, thereby succeeding in a reduction in cost of poor quality. Component traceability within supply chains can accelerate the restoration of defects. Let us suppose that a participant in supply chain finds defectives out of parts received from other participants. Component traceability systems allow the participant to automatically trace who manufactured the defective parts. As a result, the participant can receive correct parts speedily, thereby being able to quickly produce products that conform to specifications and deliver those correct products to other participants or consumers. Thus, component traceability systems can make responses to defects more swiftly than in the case of the unavailability of component traceability systems. Component traceability systems can achieve quick responses to defects and therefore reduce time to deliver goods to consumers. The shorter the time taken to reach customers, the lesser the lost sales.

For reducing the loss of sales, it is important to efficiently trace who purchased defectives in the markets through traceability systems. Retail product traceability can allow a quick response to minimize the likelihood of the occurrence of accidents due to defective products.

Hence, traceability systems for components and retail products can speed up responses to defectives. As a result, supply chains with these traceability systems can prevent consumers from having a poor image due to a delayed response to a problem caused by poor quality and, as a result, reduce lost sales. Hence, a return on investments in traceability systems within supply chains is the reduction of lost sales categorized as external failure costs.

5.4. How to promote the establishment of traceability systems

How can the promotion of the establishment of traceability systems and their beneficial uses across the overall supply chain be achieved? The solutions to the issue involve the sharing of financial information regarding the effects of capital investment in traceability systems on the shrinkage of external failure costs including reduced lost sales throughout the whole supply chain. This can help motivate all supply chain partners to aim at achieving zero-defect.

5.5. Sharing information regarding financial benefits from quality control across the supply chain

Rust *et al.* (2002) presented that financial benefits from quality are derived from revenue expansion, cost reduction, or both simultaneously. Return on quality (ROQ), calculated as profit from selling finished products divided by capital invested in quality control activities, is a combined management indicator for achieving both increasing revenue from quality improvement and decreasing cost of quality simultaneously (Rust *et al.*, 1995).

ROQ as a performance ratio for supply chain management is calculated as follows.

ROQ = Supply chains' joint profit
       ÷ the supply chains' overall quality costs comprised
         of costs from prevention and assurance activities
         and costs caused by quality failures

There are two essential approaches to increase ROQ. The first approach is to raise the supply chain's joint profit by spending more money on quality control. This method focuses on raising ROQ by generating more profit than the incremental cost of controlling its quality. However, it is difficult to match the costs incurred in quality control activities with profit earned from the quality control activities. Another approach is to achieve optimum total cost of quality by preventing quality errors effectively as well as efficiently. This method aims to contrive and execute "profitable prevention quality" activities that can reduce internal and external failure quality costs, thereby increasing profits.

An administrative point of ROQ is that supply chains must increase their joint profit by effective quality error prevention-driven minimization of total quality cost. Thus, sharing effective and efficient preventive maintenance practices among a supply chain's partners contributes to its entire profit. Moreover, putting in place a goal of supply chains' overall

ROQ can facilitate goal congruence for quality improvement across the supply chains.

When goal congruence is used, incentive alignment also needs to be applied (Bouillon *et al.*, 2006). Namely, goal congruence is linked to incentive alignment as a package of managerial practices. Incentive alignment regarding supply chain quality improvement will be examined in the next section.

6. Supply Chains' Joint Profit Sharing for Incentive Alignment

The section shows the promising effect of cost-based joint-profit allocation on quality management in supply chains. Under the cost-based allocation of a supply chain's joint profit to the participants, they can recover prevention costs incurred in them conditionally upon boosting the supply chain joint profit. Therefore, supply chain members who invested more money in quality error prevention activities can reduce rework cost, recall cost, and lost sales arising from a reputation for poor quality, thereby boosting the supply chain's joint profit. The cost-based allocation of a supply chain's joint profit aims at recovering the sum of prevention cost incurred by the partners using the supply chain's joint profit.

7. Concluding Remarks

The implementation of DFQ and DFM and the establishment of traceability systems can contribute greatly to the achievement of zero-defect and speedy responses to defectives. Consequently, supply chains are required to promote quality improvement. The issue is to motivate supply chain partners to devote their own managerial resources to quality improvement. Hence, to facilitate quality improvement across the overall supply chain, the study examined the motivational effects of sharing quality enhancement-oriented financial information based on quality costing among supply chain partners. Moreover, the study examined the impact of allocating the joint profit of a supply chain based on its quality control performance. The most effective actions for prevention quality control include those implemented at the design stage.

References

Baiman, S., Fischer, P. E., and Rajan, M. V. (2000). Information, Contracting, and Quality Costs, *Management Science*, Vol. 46, No. 6, pp. 776–789.

Beecroft, G. D. (2003). Quality Costs, in *The Executive Guide to Improvement and Change*, edited by Dennis Beecroft, G., Duffy, G. L., and Moran, J. W., Milwaukee: ASQ Quality Press, pp. 31–38.

Bouillon, M. L., Ferrier, G. D., Stuebs Jr., M. T., and West, T. D. (2006). The Economic Benefit of Goal Congruence and Implications for Management Control Systems, *Journal of Accounting and Public Policy*, Vol. 25, No. 3, pp. 265–298.

Corina, E. (2013). The Relevance of Traceability in the Food Chain, *Economics of Agriculture*, Vol. 60, No. 2, pp. 287–297.

Cowan, K., Paswan, A. K., and Steenburg, E. V. (2015). When Inter-Firm Relationship Benefits Mitigate Power Asymmetry, *Industrial Marketing Management*, Vol. 48, pp. 140–148.

FAO. (2003). *Commodities and Trade Division, Traceability Implementation in Developing Countries, Its Possibilities and Its Constraints*. A few case studies. Available at: http://docplayer.net/19198953-Traceability-implementation-in-developing-countries-its-possibilities-and-its-constraints-a-few-case-studies.html [Accessed June 15, 2018].

Feigenbaum, A. V. (1961). *Total Quality Control*, New York: McGraw-Hill.

Flynn, B. B., Schroeder, R. G., and Sakakibara, S. (1995). The Impact of Quality Management Practices on Performance and Competitive Advantage. *Decision Sciences*, Vol. 26, No. 1, pp. 659–691.

Handfield, R., Jayaram, J., and Ghosh, S. (1999). An Empirical Examination of Quality Tool Deployment Patterns and their Impact on Performance, *International Journal of Production Research*, Vol. 37, No. 6, pp. 1403–1426.

Hinckley, C. M. (1997). Defining the Best Quality-Control Systems by Design and Inspection, *Clinical Chemistry*, Vol. 43, No. 5, pp. 873–879.

Kaynak, H. (2003). The Relationship between Total Quality Management Practices and their Effects on Firm Performance, *Journal of Operations Management*, Vol. 21, No. 4, pp. 405–435.

Nandakumar, P., Datar, S. M., and Akella, R. (1993). Models for Measuring and Accounting for Cost of Conformance Quality, *Management Science*, Vol. 39, No. 1, pp. 1–16.

Obied-Allah, F. (2015). The Impact of Quality Cost on Revenue Sharing in Supply Chain Management, *International Scholarly and Scientific Research & Innovation*, Vol. 9, No. 8, pp. 2956–2966.

Rust, R. T., Moorman, C., and Dickson, P. R. (2002). Getting Return on Quality: Revenue Expansion, Cost Reduction, or Both? *Journal of Marketing*, Vol. 66, No. 4, pp. 7–24.

Rust, R. T., Zahorik, A. J., and Keiningham, T. C. (1995). Return on Quality (ROQ): Making Service Quality Financially Accountable, *Journal of Marketing*, Vol. 59, No. 2, pp. 58–70.

Taguchi, G. and Clausing, D. (1990). Robust Quality, *Harvard Business Review*, Vol. 90, No. 1, pp. 65–75.

Yamaki, K., Ando, M., and Iwaki, T. (2007). "Design to Quality" and "Design for Manufacturing" for Toshiba Notebook PCs, *Toshiba Review*, Vol. 62, No. 4, pp. 6–9 (in Japanese).

Chapter 10

Management of Humanitarian and Disaster Relief Supply Chains: Addressing Ways to Raise Funds

1. Purpose of the Study

When unfortunate disasters strike, Information and Communication Technology (ICT) can provide humanitarian supply chains with a life-safety environment. ICT can provide these supply chains with current disaster situation information to share with participants. Such ICT-driven information-sharing gives rise to effective decentralized approaches to disaster relief. Decentralization can delegate autonomous decision-making responsibility to organization members, thereby enabling them to act as swift problem-solvers. A requirement of decentralization is a shared mission among all members. Humanitarian supply chain members join for a common purpose to provide relief to disaster victims. ICT-based communications assist decentralized humanitarian supply chains and can synchronize the autonomous participant rescue operations, thereby enabling a swift response to disaster operations (Gatignon *et al.*, 2010; Nishigaki, 2011).

The main sources of revenue for humanitarian disaster-relief chains are government budgets and donations from humanitarian aid agencies and individuals. When disasters occur, potential donors are informed on how effectively these humanitarian supply chains have deployed disaster-relief aid, and accordingly make a decision on which humanitarian supply chain to donate to. Therefore, participants in a humanitarian supply chain need to work collaboratively toward delivering effective disaster-relief aid to encourage donations.

Saving human lives during emergencies, above all, requires decisive action, where the first 72 hours of a disaster are crucial (Wassenhove, 2006, p. 480). Responses to saving human lives must begin at least within that time frame, otherwise the goal of saving human lives becomes more difficult to achieve. A rapid start-up on actions to save human lives is an essential mission, and to successfully achieve this, a humanitarian supply chain is required to be self-funding. Fundraising for humanitarian relief aid comes from government budgets and donations from humanitarian aid agencies and individuals around the world. However, these funding sources are irregular, unstable and uncertain. In 2015, only 55% ($10.8 billion USD) of requested funding for humanitarian operations was met, according to the United Nations (UN) (Swithern *et al.*, 2016, p. 37). This underscores the importance of adequate funding for humanitarian supply chain operations. The study discusses a method of self-funding for rapid response operations, where respective participants in humanitarian supply chains determine the contribution they can make according to their own means. Moreover, the study addresses the advantages of online fundraising for humanitarian supply chains. This method of fundraising could be the most important source of funding for humanitarian human life-saving efforts immediately after a disaster is announced.

2. Characteristics of Humanitarian Supply Chains in Times of Disaster

Disaster management comprises of phases before and after a major emergency with pre-disaster management typically subdivided into two phases: mitigation and preparedness. The mitigation phase involves activities for constructing robust structures against disasters, such as the building of breakwaters. The preparedness phase includes community education on actions to reduce disaster risks and the contingency storage of pharmaceutical products and food. Pre-disaster management embraces the objectives of saving human life and rehabilitation (Wassenhove, 2006, pp. 480–481).

The following considers the impact of pre-disaster risk reduction activities on saving human lives by using the concept of quality costing. A managerial implication of this concept states that preventing poor quality production investments reduces poor quality production and consequently decreases total quality costs. This highlights the importance of pre-disaster risk management throughout the entire disaster-relief cycle.

One noteworthy difference between disaster relief and quality control is that while manufactures can achieve zero-defects, humans can hardly prevent the occurrence of all disasters. Furthermore, the failure of speedy relief operations in the aftermath of a disaster is one of the most critical aspects that endangers human life. This implies that humanitarian aid efforts focused on post-disaster rapid relief is as important as pre-disaster relief.

This study examines how to enhance the integration of humanitarian supply chains in the aftermath of disasters. The following discussion provides an analytical comparison between humanitarian and commercial supply chains in terms of objectives, participating entities, and methods to achieve integration and cooperation among members.

2.1. Objectivities

One significant difference between a commercial and humanitarian supply chain is the profit-seeking versus nonprofit motive. There are several missions that humanitarian relief networks achieve in the wake of a disaster, including the saving of human lives, alleviating suffering and maintaining human dignity (Good Humanitarian Donorship, 2012). To accomplish these, members are required to gather intelligence concerning information and goods needed for the rapid delivery of relief goods to disaster victims.

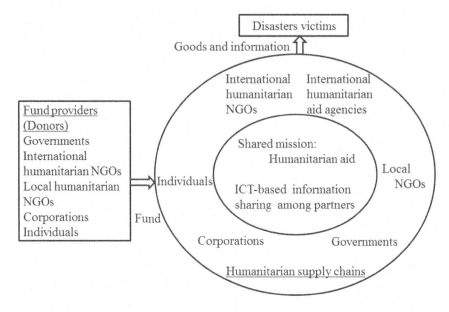

Figure 10.1.   Humanitarian supply chains (Minagawa, 2014, p. 151)

All partners in a humanitarian supply chain participate collaboratively in the network having a common mission, one of which is the provision of humanitarian disaster-relief aid (Figure 10.1).

2.2. Participating entities from different sections of business and society

A commercial supply chain essentially consists of only for-profit companies. However, a humanitarian supply chain for disaster aid comprises not only companies, but also nonprofit organizations. Participants are drawn from different communities and come together to engage in humanitarian aid activities. A humanitarian supply chain always comprises of the UN, international humanitarian nongovernmental organizations, local nongovernmental organizations, governments in disaster-affected countries, other countries, other companies, and individuals.

While a company is typically a profit-seeking entity, humanitarian aid does not include actions motivated by profit. This leads to the following question: What motivates business actors to join humanitarian supply chains, as nonprofit organizations?

According to Thomas and Fritz (2006, p. 116), a company's motivation for participating in humanitarian aid activities includes the following aspects. First, when disasters interrupt the flow of business, a company's participation in relief operations is beneficial to minimize their own economic loss. Second, corporate involvement in aid efforts is a demonstration of good corporate citizenship to various stakeholders.

An important focus for companies is achieving customer satisfaction through the supply of goods and services to markets. Commercial collaboration with relief agencies to provide humanitarian aid is beneficial for them to restart delivery of goods and services to disaster-stricken areas.

2.3. Management systems for facilitating coordination of humanitarian supply chains

A humanitarian supply chain in times of disasters is typically a hastily formed network. This network is established by participants from different sections, who usually work independently in their own areas of expertise to participate in the humanitarian aid effort. Hence, disaster-relief networks are formed by humanitarian organizations having a shared mission of aiding disaster-affected areas in times of disasters. For successful human life-saving and rehabilitation efforts, during and after the onset of a disaster, all participants in the hastily formed humanitarian relief network must collaborate and coordinate to accomplish their mission (Denning, 2006). There are several issues to overcome to achieve increasing humanitarian supply chain integration. A key success factor in supply chain management, whether humanitarian or commercial, is the method that enhances coordination and cooperation among respective partners (Xu and Beamon, 2006, p. 4; Balcik *et al.*, 2010, p. 24). To raise overall supply chain efficiency and effectiveness, it is imperative to strategically plan, build, and utilize operational interdependence among participating organizations and interaction among participants. Further, it is important to motivate participants to accept managerial decision-making leading to an increase in the supply chains' overall efficiency and effectiveness (Xu and Beamon, 2006). As participants in humanitarian relief networks are previously accustomed to working independently in their own areas of expertise, the humanitarian relief network environment experiences great difficulty in promoting coordination, relative to commercial networks.

Denning (2006) introduces *conversation spaces* to conduct a conceptual analysis on how to establish effective communication channels during a disaster. According to Denning (2006, p. 17), the *conversation space* comprises five elements; physical systems for communication, information-sharing, resource allocation, participants in humanitarian activities, and interaction practices or rules for participants to integrate their cooperation to achieve the common mission. Using *conversation spaces*, the following sections consider two factors facilitating the coordination of humanitarian supply chain efforts.

2.3.1. *Challenge to Vulnerable Predictability by Establishing ICT-Assisted Networks*

Humanitarian supply chains are exposed to an environment that is inherently more uncertain, compared to commercial supply chains, with the main objective to distribute essential goods and information to disaster-affected residents as quickly as possible. However, humanitarian supply chains in times of disasters are forced to work with greater unpredictability and uncertainty, not knowing what, who, when, and how much to supply. ICT can help humanitarian supply chains manage this uncertainty.

According to Nishigaki's study on the effects of a network on disaster relief, a communication route is subdivided into three types: an official, top-down, and private bottom-up route (Nishigaki, 2011). A study by Gatignon *et al.* (2010) showed that a humanitarian emergency aid network was better organized when operations were decentralized to manage disaster-relief activities. Gatignon *et al.* (2010) researched disaster-related response efforts led by the International Federation of Red Cross and Red Crescent Societies (IFRC), and found that IFRC's traditional centralized humanitarian supply chains had become decentralized in the last decade. An analytical comparison of decentralized and centralized humanitarian supply chains follow.

According to Gatignon *et al.* (2010), IFRC was characteristic of a centralized humanitarian supply chain until 2006. How did this centralized humanitarian supply chain manage relief operations in an interorganizational network? First, IFRC headquarters was responsible for making almost all decisions on aid operations and would organize and send a Field Assessment Coordination Team (FACT) to assess the needs of disaster-affected areas (Gatignon *et al.*, 2010, p. 103). FACT delivered this information solely to the IFRC managers upon their return. The IFRC appeared not to promote information-sharing among members committed to delivering humanitarian disaster relief, but kept information on the needs of aid recipients under its central control. Disaster-related information acquired by FACT was not updated regularly to determine a list of goods to send to disaster-affected areas, or delivered to members engaged in disaster-relief efforts (Gatignon *et al.*, 2010, p. 103). Individual members of the humanitarian network would decide what listed goods to distribute to disaster areas, rather than collectively selecting in a highly coordinated manner (Gatignon *et al.*, 2010, p. 103).

The method that IFRC traditionally acquired information was almost solely through FACT, which highlighted a key disadvantage of the traditional centralized humanitarian supply chain. This system failed to accurately capture and communicate the needs of aid recipients to all its members. This also possibly hindered use of the latest disaster-related information to drive decision-making. Consequently, such centrally controlled decision-making processes are likely to have caused failures including the unnecessary supply of goods to disaster-affected areas. Furthermore, the IFRC previously determined at their own discretion, what goods to supply to disaster-affected areas rather than a decision being based on information-sharing among all members. As a result, the IFRC often sent the same relief items to similar disaster areas (Gatignon *et al.*, 2010, p. 103).

Decentralized humanitarian supply chains can integrate and synchronize the members' operations towards increasing the effectiveness of disaster relief. Key success factors for the prompt distribution of relief include access to the latest disaster-related information, collaborative and cooperative group decision-making concerning what relief to send, identifying where to send disaster relief, and how to send relief items to aid recipients. The internet can also contribute to improving disaster-relief efforts as a network connecting humanitarian supply chains to disaster-affected regions (Minagawa, 2014).

Ensuring an enhanced performance of decentralized organizations requires cooperative integration of members' efforts. This issue will be discussed in the next section.

2.3.2. *Sharing a Common Mission among Partners*

A key factor facilitating collaboration and coordination among humanitarian supply chain partners is a shared mission to providing humanitarian relief with each participant motivated by nonprofit purpose. The existence of a shared mission is beneficial for the promotion of coordination in humanitarian relief networks, as some participants have been used to working individually and independently in different sections. To achieve the humanitarian supply chains' mission of emergency relief, partners must increase donations through the further strengthening of the humanitarian contribution to saving lives. Hence, the building and management of an effective and efficient humanitarian supply chain can improve the effectiveness of disaster-relief operations, and thereby increase donations.

Based on previous studies on supply chain management studies, one crucial factor is goal-congruence attainment among partners (Minagawa, 2010). A humanitarian supply chain consists of entities that participate and work together toward a shared purpose of providing disaster-relief efforts, resulting in a reasonably unified mission within the humanitarian supply chain. Therefore, despite being characterized as a hastily formed network that responds in times of disaster, a humanitarian supply chain does enable the building of trust immediately after the launch of relief operations (Tatham and Kovács, 2010, p. 39). This stems from all participants' perception that they belong to a network that is unified by a common goal (Minagawa, 2014).

3. A Framework for Analyzing Humanitarian Supply Chain Management

3.1. Fundraising for relief aid operations

While the major source of revenue for commercial supply chains is through customer payment in exchange for goods and services rendered, fundraising for humanitarian relief aid comes from government budgets and donations from humanitarian aid agencies and individuals.

More importantly, the uncertainty of government budgets and funding for humanitarian relief agencies or donations for disaster-relief aid means that ongoing humanitarian supply chain funding is typically unstable.

3.2. Performance evaluation

Business performance of a commercial supply chain is determined by a market response to goods supplied and the market reputation of the supply chain affects its profitability. Humanitarian supply chain performance is evaluated differently by the international community. Success is measured in terms of success in saving lives and alleviating suffering in disaster-affected areas. As a result, the reputation of humanitarian relief networks has an impact on the budget allocation for disaster-relief efforts authorized by governments and the amount of donations received from humanitarian aid agencies and individuals.

3.3. Achieving humanitarian aid effectively and efficiently to increase funding

As an increase in revenue leads to company growth, similarly an increase in funding, including donations, to a humanitarian supply chain leads to increased contributions towards disaster relief. To continually improve relief operations, humanitarian supply chains must spend increased funding and demonstrate operational success as a positive rate of return to contributors. This can further enhance their reputation in the international community.

While companies generate revenues from offering attractive products and services to customers, a humanitarian supply chain's funding source includes government funding and donations from various humanitarian aid organizations. When donors assess which humanitarian supply chain to support, they follow the rule of best value for money. Central to enhancing the humanitarian supply chains' reputation in the international community is the goal of distributing the right relief goods to the right recipients at the right time and in the right quantity.

4. A Conceptual Roadmap for Effective Humanitarian Supply Chains

Below is a conceptual roadmap for the establishment of effective humanitarian relief supply chains as explained in this study.

- Rapid formulation of humanitarian supply chains at the onset of a disaster
↓

- Accelerate fundraising for rapid start-up of initial responses to disasters using partners' cooperative fund contributions and crowdfunding
↓

- Apply management systems to successfully integrate participants into the supply chain to achieve life-saving and disaster relief
↓

- Gain a reputation among donors internationally through fundraising for rapid start-up of initial responses to disaster events and employment of integration management systems
↓

- Resulting increase in disaster-relief funds

4.1. Importance of rapid start-up of initial responses to save human lives

To save lives during a natural disaster, humanitarian supply chains need to quickly launch an initial response at the early stage of an emergency. Rapid initial response start-ups strongly induces donations in the following manner. As a disaster occurs, potential donors begin a decision-making process concerning which humanitarian supply chains to donate to. For example, while potential donors may have been considering where to donate, a certain humanitarian supply chain promptly launches an initial response to a human-life-saving situation which is communicated to potential donors through the media. Such media reports enable a humanitarian supply chain to attract more donors.

A successful early initial start-up operation for saving human lives can strengthen disaster-relief contributions. However, humanitarian supply chains are inevitably confronted with the issue of how to fund prompt initial startup responses, which is subsequently explored.

4.2. Partners' voluntary cooperative fund contribution according to their respective means for funding quick start-up of initial response

Any humanitarian supply chain faces uncertainty regarding whether it will succeed in raising funds in the aftermath of a disaster. Notwithstanding the fact that rapid start-up of initial responses to saving lives strengthens disaster-relief contributions, humanitarian supply chains are required to resolve fundraising issues in the initial stage of a disaster. One effective way for securing funds is the application of a partners' voluntary contribution fund in which the fundraising process proceeds in the following manner.

As a disaster occurs, participants in a humanitarian supply chain collaboratively formulate a plan of initial disaster-relief response and estimate necessary funds for the disaster-relief efforts. A key success factor in partners' self-funding is the appropriate selection method for determining the amount of money to be offered by respective partners. Since humanitarian supply chains are not-for-profit organizations, it is important to introduce a contribution method in which respective partners voluntarily determine the amount of contribution they can make. Funds contributed by partners are characteristic of internal funds of a humanitarian supply chain. This self-funded money can then be applied to initial disaster responses with potential donors informed through the media, thereby increasing donations to the humanitarian supply chain.

4.3. The impacts of crowdfunding on humanitarian disaster relief

4.3.1. *Effects of Crowdfunding*

The raising of more money for humanitarian supply chains can significantly improve the performance of rescue operations. As the need to boost donations is ever present, this section will discuss the advantages of online donations.

On March 11, 2011, a magnitude 9.0 earthquake caused a huge tsunami that struck Northeast Japan. At the time as this disaster, the internet served as a powerful donation tool (Saxton and Zhuang, 2013, p. 42). In the first 5 days after the earthquake, the American Red Cross (ARC) received $34 million in donation to support relief operations (Strom, 2011). A large number of those donations received in the first few days were believed to be sent via the Internet.

Crowdfunding is a new model used by individuals and organizations to fund projects, mostly via the internet, by soliciting monetary contributions from people all over the world (Belleflamme *et al.*, 2014). Crowdfunding promotes financing via a web-based platform and serves as a swift information dissemination tool linking prospective donors and fundraisers. It can also act as a powerful financial instrument connecting donors to fundraisers on a global scale. There are two types of crowdfunding: donation-based and reward-based. Donation-based crowdfunding involves contributors who support a specific project. This model differs from reward-based crowdfunding where investors expect financial returns in exchange for investing in projects. This study explains the benefits of crowdfunding to raise funds for a humanitarian disaster-relief network to successfully provide disaster relief.

Based on Meyskens and Bird (2015, p. 157), the following explains the process of donation-based crowdfunding. The first step is establishing a humanitarian supply chain to provide disaster relief. This humanitarian disaster-relief network then selects a web-based platform in the crowdfunding market and is then used to solicit disaster-relief contributions and accept donations. The crowdfunding platform is a tool used to communicate fundraising-specific disclosure information and accept payment of money. Crowdfunding platforms require fundraisers to reimburse a fixed fee or a fee proportional to the total amount of money raised. The humanitarian supply chain then applies money raised towards relief projects. To ensure accountability, the disaster aid network also delivers information to donors about raised funds, including the final uses of donated money.

The greatest benefit of using online-based crowdfunding lies in the acceleration of the financing process as it is essential for humanitarian supply chains to quickly raise funds to provide disaster relief. Online fundraising can deliver donation requests globally and contributors can easily make payments via web-based fundraising sites. As a result, the application of internet-based fundraising by humanitarian disaster-relief chains can accelerate securing donation targets. According to Nunnenkamp and Öhler (2013, p. 83), the fundraising activities of NGOs is a nonproductive operational exercise and reduces time away from engaging in humanitarian relief activities.

The effects of internet-based fundraising on humanitarian supply chains are as follows. Humanitarian supply chains can accelerate fundraising online, resulting in freeing up more time to dedicate towards providing disaster-relief aid. This can improve the performance of humanitarian supply chain relief aid operations. The acceleration of fundraising efforts, via the internet, further enhances the credibility of humanitarian supply chains amongst the international community. The perceived community higher value toward a humanitarian supply chain is the single most important success driver to capture competitive advantages in competition with other humanitarian relief networks.

4.3.2. *Core Advantage of Internet-Assisted Crowdfunding for Humanitarian Supply Chains*

The global utilization and prevalence of the Internet is well known. ICT-assisted communication tools allow people over the world to capture relief aid activities by humanitarian supply chains in the aftermath of a disaster. Local communities can easily access crowdfunding options online, recognize humanitarian supply chain disaster aid activities in place and make a donation.

Therefore, internet-assisted crowdfunding systems enable communities to donate immediately after recognizing the disaster-relief activities of humanitarian supply chains. The internet can assist the expansion of humanitarian supply chain fund raising.

4.4. Effectiveness of partners' voluntary cooperative self-funding

A discussion of partners' voluntary cooperative fund contributions provides a valuable insight into the liquidity profile of partners. Contribution arrangements among partners assumes a shared risk. This funding mechanism, where partners fund and assume the risk of initial disaster-relief operations, is not always successful. However, this risk-sharing among participants in humanitarian supply chains is helpful to increase coordination and cooperation efforts from the following perspective.

A key control for an interorganizational network is the management of mutual organizational relationships and coordination of interdependent actions conducted by partners. It is also important for humanitarian supply chains to create well-coordinated and highly cooperative partnerships conducive to increasing donations through strengthening humanitarian disaster aid contributions.

As in Simatupang *et al.* (2002, p. 291), coordination among participants in an inter-firm network including a supply chain has two analytical perspectives: the mutuality of coordination and the focus of coordination. The mutuality norm suggests that a partner's collective responsibility towards successfully building a sustainable growing network contributes to stronger and closer relationships among partners (Simatupang *et al.*, 2002, p. 292). Moreover, successful sharing of joint responsibility for increased overall network performance requires dissemination of common understandings across organizational borders (Simatupang *et al.*, 2002, p. 292). Examples that help generate common understandings in an inter-firm network include sharing of information and goal-congruence. The focus of coordination covers areas from the activities conducted by each partner to partners' business administration methods (Simatupang *et al.*, 2002, p. 293).

By focusing on the management of humanitarian supply chains, the partners' voluntary cooperative contribution fund for self-funding initial disaster response promotes risk-sharing as well as joint responsibility for increasing donations, thereby strengthening the sense of unity among members.

5. Summary

Fundraising for humanitarian relief aid comes from government budgets and donations from aid agencies and individuals around the world. These funding sources are irregular, unstable and uncertain. Raising funds to achieve a rapid start-up of an initial response to save lives poses a significant difficulty for humanitarian supply chains. Humanitarian supply chains mostly depend on self-funding in the early stages of the disaster cycle. Moreover, the use online-crowdfunding is important in supporting rapid initial disaster response.

References

Balcik, B., Beamon, B. M., Krejci, C. C., Muramatsu, K. M., and Ramirez, M. (2010). Coordination in Humanitarian Relief Chains: Practices, Challenges and Opportunities, *International Journal of Production Economics*, Vol. 126, No. 1, pp. 22–34.

Belleflamme, P., Lambert, T., and Schwienbacher, A. (2014). Crowdfunding: Tapping the Right Crowd, *Journal of Business Venturing*, Vol. 29, No. 5, pp. 585–609.

Denning, P. J. (2006). Hastily Formed Networks, *Communication of the ACM*, Vol. 49, No. 4, pp. 15–20.

Gatignon, A., Wassenhove, L. N. V., and Charles, A. (2010). The Yogyakarta Earthquake: Humanitarian Relief Through IFRC's Decentralized Supply Chain, *International Journal of Production Economics*, Vol. 126, No. 1, pp. 102–110.

Good Humanitarian Donorship (2012). Available at: https://www.ghdinitiative. org/ghd/gns/home-page.html [Accessed June 15, 2018].

Meyskens, M. and Bird, L. (2015). Crowdfunding and Value, *The Entrepreneurship Research Journal*, Vol. 5, No. 2, pp. 155–166.

Minagawa, Y. (2010). How Can Management Accounting Achieve Goal Congruence among Supply Chain Partners, in *Business Group Management in Japan*, edited by Hamada, K., Singapore: World Scientific Publishing Co., pp. 121–136.

Minagawa, Y. (2014). Management of Humanitarian Supply Chains in Times of Disaster, in *Management of Enterprise Crises in Japan*, edited by Monden, Y., Singapore: World Scientific Publishing Co., pp. 149–163.

Nishigaki, T. (2011). Decentralized Approaches to Natural Disaster Management, "Economic Column" Series on the Role of Internet-Based Systems in Effective Natural Disaster Management, May 3, 2011, Nikkei Shimbun.

Nunnenkamp, P. and Öhler, H. (2013). Funding, Competition and the Efficiency of NGOs: An Empirical Analysis of Non-charitable Expenditure of US NGOs Engaged in Foreign Aid, *KYKLOS*, Vol. 65, No. 1, pp. 81–110.

Saxton, G. D. and Zhuang, J. (2013). A Game-Theoretic Model of Disclosure-Donation Interactions in the Market for Charitable Contributions, *Journal of Applied Communication Research*, Vol. 41, No. 1, pp. 40–63.

Simatupang, T. M., Wright, A. C., and Sridharan, R. (2002). The Knowledge of Coordination for Supply Chain Integration, *Business Process Management Journal*, Vol. 8, No. 3, pp. 289–308.

Strom, S. (2011). A Charitable Rush, With Little Direction, *New York Times*, March 16, p. A14.

Swithern, S., Lattimer, C., Sparks, D., Tuchel, L., Caio, C., Beecher, J., Collins, R., Dalrymple, S., Galinie, A., Kenei, S., Knox, D., Miller, A., Shaikh, L., Simenon, M., Parrish, C., Tew, R., Watts, R., and Wasiuk, D. (2016). *Global Humanitarian Assistance Report 2016*, Tech. Rep., Global Humanitarian Assistance.

Tatham, P. and Kovács, G. (2010). The Application of "Swift Trust" to Humanitarian Logistics, *International Journal of Production Economics*, Vol. 126, No. 1, pp. 35–45.

Thomas, A. and Fritz, L. (2006). Disaster Relief, Inc., *Harvard Business Review*, Vol. 84 (November), pp. 114–122.

Wassenhove, L. N. V. (2006). Blackett Memorial Lecture: Humanitarian Aid Logistics: Supply Chain Management in High Gear, *Journal of the Operational Research Society*, Vol. 57, No. 5, pp. 475–489.

Xu, L. and Beamon, B. M. (2006). Supply Chain Coordination and Cooperation Mechanisms: An Attribute-Based Approach, *The Journal of Supply Chain Management*, Vol. 42, No. 1 (Winter), pp. 4–12.

Index

A

absorption costing, 104
activity-based costing (ABC), 84
activity-based life-cycle costing
   (ABLCC), 119
appraisal costs, 131
Asanuma, 64, 80, 89

B

balanced scorecard, 7, 48
bargaining power, 66
Black and Scholes, 36
break-even time (BET), 12, 17,
   115–116, 119
brick-and-mortar shops, 53

C

call option, 36
Clark and Fujimoto, 18, 116
collaboration performance system
   (CPS), 13
conformity to requirement
   or specification, 130
cost leadership, 88

cost to serve (CTS), 114, 122–123
crowdfunding, 156
customer accounting, 113–114
customer perspective, 50, 57
customer satisfaction, 52
customer value, 14

D

DA parts suppliers, 93–94
design for manufacturability (DFM),
   134, 136–138
design for quality (DFQ), 134,
   136–138
design to life-cycle cost, 117
design to price (DTP), 21, 23
differentiation, 88
donation-based crowdfunding,
   156
drawing approved (DA) parts
   suppliers, 80
drawing approved suppliers, 64
drawing supplied (DS) parts
   suppliers, 64, 80
DS parts, 89, 91

E
electronics manufacturing service (EMS), 64, 68, 72
external failure costs, 132

F
fabless firms, 64, 68, 72
fabless supply chains, 65, 74
financial perspective, 56
focus, 88
Fujimoto, 93
functional product, 113
functional shiftability, 85, 126

G
growth and learning perspective, 58
growth-share matrix, 101

H
humanitarian disaster-relief chains, 146
humanitarian supply chains, 145

I
innovative products, 113
internal and external failure quality costs, 140
internal failure costs, 131

K
Kaplan and Anderson, 125
Kaplan and Norton, 7, 48–49

L
lean consumption, 121
learning cost, 26
life-cycle cost, 15, 116
life-cycle costing, 119

M
Makido, 16, 21
market price-based transfer pricing, 72, 93
minimum efficient scale (MES), 90
Monden, 5, 16, 71, 84
multistage real options, 39

N
National Football League, 3
new sales ratio (NSR), 25

P
partners' voluntary cooperative fund contribution, 155
porter, 2, 79, 88
prevention costs, 131
product life cycle, 6, 11
product portfolio, 100
product portfolio management (PPM), 115

Q
quality costing, 130
quality costs, 131

R
relationship-specific investments, 31, 70
return on quality (ROQ), 140
revenue sharing, 3
reward-based crowdfunding, 156

S
supply chain risk, 32
supply chain system perspective, 57
switching costs, 26, 70
switching partners, 8
switching partnerships, 73

T
target costing, 15
target pricing-driven NPD, 22
technical dialogue, 67
technology life cycle, 63
throughput accounting, 103, 105
time-based activity cost, 125
time-to-market (TTM), 12, 115–116, 120
Toyota, 84
traceability, 133
traceability systems, 134–135, 139
transfer pricing, 93
transfer pricing based on throughput accounting, 106
twin security, 38

V
value-based pricing, 19
variable (direct) costing, 104
vendor-managed inventory (VMI), 85
vertically integrated firm, 63

W
Williamson, 31
Womack and Jones, 121

Z
zero-defect, 129

Printed in the United States
By Bookmasters